KILLER UX DESIGN

BY JODIE MOULE

Killer UX Design

by Jodie Moule

Copyright © 2012 SitePoint Pty. Ltd.

Product Manager: Simon Mackie   **Editor:** Kelly Steele

Technical Editor: Diana MacDonald   **Cover Designer:** Alex Walker

Expert Reviewer: Matt Magain

Indexer: Fred Brown

Printing History:

   September 2012

sitepoint

Published by SitePoint Pty. Ltd.

48 Cambridge Street Collingwood
VIC Australia 3066
Web: www.sitepoint.com
Email: business@sitepoint.com

ISBN 978-0-9871530-9-8 (print)

ISBN 978-0-9872478-0-3 (ebook)
Printed and bound in the United States of America

About Jodie Moule

Jodie Moule is co-founder and director of Symplicit, an experience design consultancy based in Australia that focuses on research, strategy, and design services. With a background in psychology, her understanding of human behavior is central to helping businesses see their brands through the eyes of customers, influencing the way they approach the design of their products, systems, and processes.

About SitePoint

SitePoint specializes in publishing practical, rewarding, and approachable content for web professionals. Visit http://www.sitepoint.com/ to access our books, blogs, newsletters, videos, and community forums.

To my best friend, business partner, husband, and father of our wonderful children, Blake and Darci. This is for you Steve, because without you, it would not have been possible. Love you lots.

To Blake and Darci, I wonder what the future holds? Hold on tight and make the most of every moment. Love Mummy.

Table of Contents

Chapter 4   Making Sense of What You've Found 83

Chapter 5   Sketching to Explore the Design Concept 117

Chapter 7   Test, Learn, Tweak. Iterate 191

Chapter 8   Launch to Learn About Behavior

Preface

When I embarked on my career as a psychologist, I never imagined I'd end up designing technology products and services. Funny where you end up in life, and lucky for me all those years at university weren't wasted: the business of understanding humans and the way they behave is critical to designing.

With the digital and physical worlds merging more than ever before, it is vital to understand how technology can enhance the human experience, and not cause frustration or angst at every touchpoint.

To create technology that seamlessly fits into our daily lives, there's a simple formula. First, consider the person attached to your technology solution and the context in which they'll be using your creation; then, design your solution and involve users in the process to refine your thinking.

Today, technology is used to change attitudes and behavior, creating amazing challenges for designers. And if we want to create products and services that have the power to educate people so that they may live better lives, or help to reduce the time people take to do certain tasks—or even attract them to our products instead of our competitors—we need to first understand what makes them tick.

User-friendliness is fast becoming a necessity in product design. Nevertheless, we still have a long way to go to deliver on our users' (high) expectations, and this will only increase as technology and the real world continue to merge.

Understanding behavior allows us to change the customer experience, and that change happens through great design—your great designs.

What is this book about?

This book aims to be an introduction to user experience design. UX design is an approach that starts by understanding the behavior of the eventual users of a product, service, or system. It then seeks to explore the optimal interaction of these elements, in order to design experiences that are memorable, enjoyable, and a little bit "wow."

The premise of this book is the need to understand how people behave (their habits, motivators, and drivers) to make well-informed design decisions that produce a great customer experience for your users.

Case Study to Bring It All to Life

Depending on the type of business problem you are solving and the product you are designing, there are several ways to approach a design problem. To bring the theory to life, I'll be presenting a case study so you can see the theory discussed in each chapter applied to a real-life example. It's my intention that through this example, you'll see the benefits a UX process can bring to your projects.

I encourage you to think about what you would have done if this project was thrust upon you at work, or if a client approached you to deliver an app as a way to help enhance your learning as you read along.

Who Should Read This Book

This book was written for people who have heard of UX and want to learn more about the basics, or expand their knowledge on distinct aspects of the UX process. If you are charged with understanding how to apply a UX process to your projects, but are unsure quite where to start—this book is for you.

My aim was to present UX design in a fun, practical, and non-academic way, so that the concepts are accessible and can be tried out immediately. In this regard, this book is for newcomers to the UX space rather than seasoned professionals. However, those with a UX background and some experience might be interested to see how we approached design problems.

What's in This Book

The book contains the following eight chapters:

Chapter 1: *You Are Not Your User*
> This chapter defines UX design and considers what makes a great experience. You'll learn why this should matter to you when designing.

Chapter 2: *Understand the Business Problem*

If you're unable to understand the problem, you can't solve it. This chapter explores the problem that your client or company aims to solve with the UX process, and explains some useful ways to ensure your for success.

Chapter 3: *Understand the User Context*

In order to produce great usable designs, you need to gain empathy and understanding for your users. We'll address all the research methods available to you and look at how to recruit users for testing.

Chapter 4: *Making Sense of What You've Found*

In this chapter, we discuss how to analyze the data you've collected from your user testing. Then we'll delve into behavior design and reveal why understanding behavior and habits is intrinsic to your design work.

Chapter 5: *Sketching to Explore the Design Concept*

Once we've conducted an analysis, we move towards using sketching as a tool. Sketching is cost-effective and easy to do, and helps to generate lots of ideas quickly so that you can select a few really great ones to take to the next stage.

Chapter 6: *Prototype the Solution*

Forming working models of your design is the best way to assess whether your solution—once imagined beyond paper—is going to work or not. Creating rapid prototypes to refine your thought process and ensure you're on the right track is a critical step in your UX process.

Chapter 7: *Test, Learn, Tweak. Iterate*

The whole reason for creating prototypes is to test them with your users, in order to validate whether your design is worth pursuing. This process allows you to ascertain whether users understand your design, and allows for further refining. Final tweaks now will give you confidence that the decisions you've made along the way are the right ones.

Chapter 8: *Launch to Learn About Behavior*

This final chapter focuses on testing and evaluating your solution as you prepare to launch—and beyond. Once you've let it loose on the market, you'll continue to learn from users' habits and behaviors as they use your product, bringing your UX process full circle .

Where to Find Help

Design is an evolving area, so chances are good that by the time you read this, some minor detail or other of these technologies will have changed from what's described in this book. Thankfully, SitePoint has a thriving community of designers ready and waiting to help you out if you run into trouble. We also maintain a list of known errata for this book that you can consult for the latest updates.

The SitePoint Forums

The SitePoint Forums[1] are discussion forums where you can ask questions about anything related to web design and development. You may, of course, answer questions, too. A lot of fun and experienced web designers and developers hang out there, and it's a good way to learn new stuff, have questions answered in a hurry, and just have fun. In particular, check out the design thread.

The Book's Website

Located at http://www.sitepoint.com/books/ux1/, the website that supports this book will give you access to the following facilities:

Tools

As you progress through this book, you'll note that we've performed a number of user testing sessions. See the book's website to access the documents and templates we've made available to support you in your own user sessions.

Updates and Errata

No book is perfect, and we expect that alert readers will be able to spot at least one or two mistakes before the end of this one. The Errata page on the book's website will always have the latest information about known typographical and code errors.

The SitePoint Newsletters

In addition to books like this one, SitePoint publishes free email newsletters such as the *SitePoint* newsletter, *PHPMaster*, *CloudSpring*, *RubySource*, *DesignFestival*, and *BuildMobile*. In them you'll read about the latest news, product releases, trends,

---

[1] http://www.sitepoint.com/forums/

tips, and techniques for all aspects of web development. Sign up to one or more of these newsletters at http://www.sitepoint.com/newsletter/.

Your Feedback

If you've downloaded the app, we'd love to hear your thoughts on it and any ideas that we may not have considered. Get in touch at `hello@symplicit.com.au`, or on Twitter: @jodiemoule and @thecookapp.

For SitePoint, if you're unable to find an answer through the forums or wish to contact us for any other reason, the best place to write is `books@sitepoint.com`. We have an email support system set up to track inquiries, and if our support crew are unable to answer your question, they'll send it straight to us. Suggestions for improvements, as well as notices of any mistakes you may find, are welcome.

Acknowledgments

Writing this book has been one of the most rewarding—and challenging—things I have ever bitten off in my career. I'd like to thank the SitePoint team who I got to know over the course of nearly a year, namely Simon, Matt, and Tom during the writing process, with Di and Kelly during the edits. Thanks guys for being there as I agonized about chapters and made false starts, all while gently reminding me to meet deadlines (ugh!).

I really want to thank the app team that made it possible to deliver the case-study app we created: Cook. I think we can safely say that the app has turned into something bigger than we imagined. A special note goes to my fellow Cook business partners and directors: Stephen Moule, Alex Johnston, and Jeff Tan-Ang. Thanks for believing in the idea, guys. I couldn't have done it without you, and have had (and am still having) a ball in the process. The sleepless nights and lack of weekends are all worth it … honest!

To our team members Jamie Chin, Ekaterina Vasilenko, Chris Michelle-Wells, and Jonathan Sagorin—the Cook app team who were involved at each stage of the UX process, and who worked tirelessly on the app. An extra special thanks goes to Stephen, Jamie, and Ekat for working back late and on weekends to design all the amazing images and posters for this book; and to Chris and Ekat for finalizing and perfecting the videos—you guys rock! I can't thank you enough.

Thanks, too, goes to the Symplicit team for tolerating my absence from day-to-day business for nearly a year, and stepping in to keep things running smoothly. Guys, as a group, I owe you all a great big thanks for your support during this time.

Thanks to my dearly departed Grandmother and parents for seeding a love of cooking, and therefore being the source of what we thought was a great design idea for the case study. Cook is for foodies like you, Mum and Dad; now I just need to get you both onto an iPad so that you can use it!

Most of all, the biggest thanks goes to my beloved husband, Stephen, who managed our business in my absence, and looked after our kids weekends, early mornings, and late at night for close to a year, as I worked to get this book completed. And still managed to smile and be a wonderful husband and father despite it all. Thanks honey. Without you, Blake, and Darci, there is nothing. You are my world.

Conventions Used in This Book

You'll notice that we've used certain typographic and layout styles throughout this book to signify different types of information. Look out for the following items.

Tips, Notes, and Warnings

Hey, You!

Tips will give you helpful little pointers.

Ahem, Excuse Me ...

Notes are useful asides that are related—but not critical—to the topic at hand. Think of them as extra tidbits of information.

Make Sure You Always ...

... pay attention to these important points.

Watch Out!

Warnings will highlight any gotchas that are likely to trip you up along the way.

You Are Not Your User

So what is user experience (UX) anyway?

You might think it would be a relatively easy term to define; however, when I reflected on the evolution of UX, it was quite a difficult task. Why?

UX covers a broad range of interactions a person can have with a business, and in an increasingly connected world, the lines are blurring between the digital and nondigital spheres. What might begin as an online experience can extend into a physical interaction (say, in a bricks-and-mortar store) and then be further influenced with an instore representative—all shaped by a particular business process.

A Broad Perspective

So, let's attempt a simple explanation. **User experience (UX)** is the sum of a series of interactions a person has with a product, service, or organization. A general example of all these elements interacting can be seen in Figure 1.1.

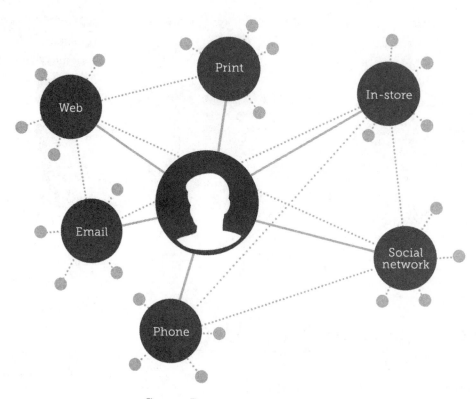

Figure 1.1. The sum of a series of interactions

Broadly considering a user's lifestyle and the overall context of how a product or service is used is necessary if you want to improve on the experience you deliver. This is especially true of digital experiences, and, nowadays, they are closely linked to other channels. To the end-user (or customer), the UX you provide will reflect their perceived experience with your brand, whether dealing with your company online, via a mobile app, or talking to your call center.

The term "user experience" was coined by Don Norman while he was vice president of the Advanced Technology Group at Apple in the 1990s. Upon coming up with the term, Norman said: "I thought human interface and usability were too narrow. I wanted to cover all aspects of the person's experience with the system, including industrial design graphics, the interface, the physical interaction, and the manual. Since then the term has spread widely, so much so that it is starting to lose its meaning."[1]

---

[1] You can read an excerpt of this interview, or listen to the full hour-long conversation [http://www.adaptivepath.com/ideas/e000862] with Don Norman, a luminary in the field of UX.

As Don implies, it's easy enough to let the term "UX" roll off the tongue, but many people lack an appreciation of what it means to deliver the broader aspects of UX, instead taking a narrow approach and considering only one or two elements.

Embracing Multidisciplinary Teams

UX embraces a multidisciplinary approach: the method of using multiple perspectives when tackling a design issue to lead to the best outcomes.

UX incorporates contributions from many disciplines, including:

- interaction design
- human factors engineering (HFE)
- industrial design
- psychology
- anthropology
- sociology
- computer science
- graphic design
- cognitive science

Generally speaking, UX combines all these elements, and covers both digital and nondigital experiences. Designing for user-product experiences that occur nondigitally is often referred to as **experience design**, with the term **customer experience** sometimes used to refer to the sum total of interactions a person has with a brand. Even defining what a customer is can cause confusion among industries; for example, marketing departments might view a customer experience differently from how an industrial designer does.

In this book, we'll focus on a process that can be used across your projects, helping you to create a seamless interaction between your user and your product (whether it's software or hardware). I will assume that your projects are digitally based, though the UX process we'll be examining can also be applied to designing offline products and services just as effectively.

As UX has become more of a buzzword, I've noticed that many people believe "user experience" only applies to interface design. More than assessing a product's ease of use, UX as a philosophy puts the end-user's needs at the center of the design and development process. It's about understanding and prioritizing those needs before, during, and after any interaction a user has with a company. This switches the traditional IT approach where technology drives decisions. Too often, technology projects have failed because they haven't been designed to anticipate the type of person that will ultimately use the system, as well as the context in which they'll use it.

What makes an experience?

There are several factors that affect the overall experience a user has with a product:

- Usefulness: is the product useful, with a clear purpose?

- Usability: is the product easy to use—navigating within and interacting with—and requiring little need for guidance?

- Learnability: is the product simple to master quickly with minimal instruction required?

- Aesthetics: is the visual appearance of the product and its design appealing to the user?

- Emotions: are the emotional feelings evoked in response to the product and the brand positive, and do they have a lasting impact on the user and their willingness to use the product?

When you consider this range of potential influences, it's easy to see why many disciplines come together to design and deliver a holistic UX.

You've Got to Have a Method

In the field of UX, we examine users' needs with a series of contextual methods known as a **User-centered Design (UCD) methodology**. This is a framework that enables us to engage with and listen to our users to determine what they want. UCD is a design approach that considers a user's needs up front and throughout the design and development process, in order to ensure that the final product is well received. In this book, we'll step through what is essentially the application of UCD practices to generate designs that consider a more integrated UX.

The method we'll follow is outlined in Figure 1.2, where we'll move from a **research phase** (understanding the problem and the user context) through to interpreting

insights (making sense of what you've found). Then we'll progress to the **concept stage** (sketching, prototyping, and iterating your designs, as well as involving users in this process to validate your approach). Finally, we will move into the **design experience** (where you implement the final product, and monitor and improve it over time).

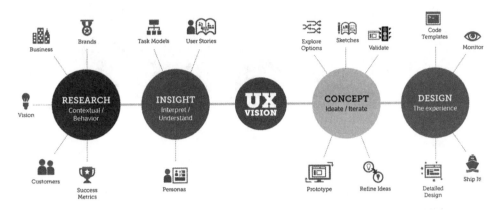

Figure 1.2.

This process will be brought to life through the case study of developing a cooking app, where we'll use techniques that are unique to each stage.

The Cost of Overlooking Your Users

I often hear people say they lack the time to involve users, but plenty of projects have bombed because they've failed to consider the user in the design and development process. The earlier that users likely to be using your products evaluate your designs, the less likely it is you'll have to go back and rework them. The expense of learning this only when you've already launched your product is enormous. Time and money will be saved if you step in early and evaluate your design with end-users, understanding what it's like for them to use the product way before the final design or code is even considered, as depicted in Figure 1.3. This step is essential to success.

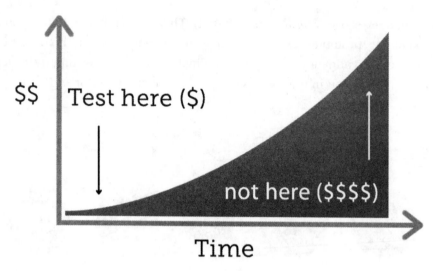

Figure 1.3. The cost savings of UX

Many of the methods commonly used in a UX process are qualitative in nature rather than quantitative. We'll cover learning about behavior in the section called "Understanding Human Behavior" in Chapter 2, but to summarize:

qualitative research
> looks at users' actual behaviors in order to gain an in-depth understanding of the how and why of human decision-making (habits and behaviors)

quantitative research
> focuses on mass data collection and the analysis of themes to derive assumptions around human behavior; statistically based, this gives more of a sense of what, where, and when (attitudes and self-reported motivators)

Usually, qualitative research requires a much smaller sample size than its data-driven counterpart. (Quantitative research is often derived through large-scale market research surveys that cover big sample sizes, with numbers usually into the thousands.) This is good news for your design and development activities, as insights gathered from a few users are quick and easy to obtain, and will improve your approach to work if gathered early and often throughout the process. Understanding behavior is the first step toward influencing or changing the way your users perform tasks; whether you've thought about it previously or not, this change is brought about through your design work.

A Balanced Approach to Solving Problems

In UX, we're led by user needs (desirability) as a way of driving the creation of products and services, but this is counterbalanced by feasibility (can it be done?) and viability (does it make sense to the business?). Remember, our users don't have all the answers. While they're great for informing and testing our design concepts, they should never provide the sole basis of a business decision. Take a look at where to start and where to aim for in Figure 1.4.

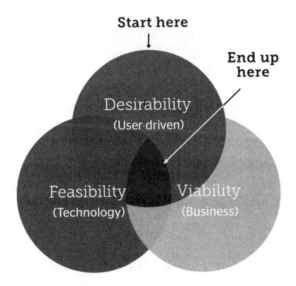

Figure 1.4. Start with desirability first

Once we have gathered insights into our target users, the job of assessing overall feasibility and viability must be reviewed in light of what the business is capable of delivering. The most successful product design understands the balance between user, business, and technological needs; therefore, taking a UX approach requires an understanding of a business landscape that is broader than the project we are engaged to deliver. Exposure to products and services across various areas of an organization helps us to design end-to-end experiences that are a pleasure to use, and you may also identify areas where business costs can be reduced. This often means communicating across different departments or disciplines—IT, marketing, branding, product areas, and so on—in order to realize the best outcomes.

UCD methods have long been a foundation to what's often referred to as **design thinking**. Design thinking is essentially about:

- being human-centered so as to be empathetic to your audience

- **ideating**, the process of thinking through multiple options and solutions for a given problem

- using prototypes as a way to help you work through design problems

- being process-sensitive and understanding that a client's products and services comprise many parts that form a whole

Design thinking is an overall process that consists of rapidly coming up with ideas, testing concepts, and getting feedback from real users, all while refining your approach. This is UX in a nutshell.

Adopting this plan of attack on your projects will guarantee that you're pulling your ideas together quickly, making informed choices, evaluating and reviewing your ideas with others, and gathering feedback early and often from the product's end-users. All this works to ensure that you'll succeed once you've gone live. Rather than the user dictating outcomes, it helps you—the design expert—to think about the problem at hand, allowing your ideas to evolve as you move through the stages of a design. Perhaps this is different to what you thought constituted a UX approach, but I hope it reveals how you can balance user feedback with your own ideas in order to attain the best design solution in a structured way.

Put Yourself in the User's Shoes

Two factors essential to a successful UX approach are:

- considering the person will eventually use your product

- thinking about the context that the product might be used within

Ultimately, this is about having empathy. I quite often find myself thinking: "How would my parents react to this product?" To me, they represent average, everyday users, and are a good litmus test for whether my designs will be well-received by a broader audience. My parents are like the majority of people not working in IT or any technical industry: they are not highly tech-savvy, but find themselves being pushed into the digital world more and more by companies that are looking for ways to service clients more efficiently and cost-effectively. Like most users I've talked to over the years, my parents hesitate when they are confronted with new technology for the first time; they worry about breaking something by pressing the wrong button, and have relayed stories of becoming lost while downloading an ebook.

Here's what I've learned, working in our labs and with people: users do a range of crazy, unexpected things with the interfaces we design, and design patterns we believe are easy to understand are sometimes unclear. Over the years, I've listened as users blame themselves when they find a product difficult to use, shrugging to themselves that "they'll get used to it."

This type of behavior has been observed and reported upon for years now within the UX industry, and so it is sometimes surprising that we still see this type of learned helplessness rearing its head in our user-focused research.[2]

In your design work, it's essential to have empathy for the end-users of your product, and this is more easily achieved working in the UX field than you might think. You'll often come up against regular reality checks. Ultimately, it's not the user's fault if they can't make a system work; it is our responsibility as designers to get it right for them, and to make it as easy as possible for them to perform the tasks they want to do. As indicated in Figure 1.5, you need to put yourself in their shoes.

---

[2] For more on learned helplessness, see the foundational research into the conditioning of dogs that were repeatedly hurt by an adverse stimulus they could not escape, until they eventually stopped trying to avoid the pain. This became referred to as "learned helplessness" due to the their inability to change the situation. Maier, S.F. and Seligman, M.E.P., "Learned Helplessness: Theory and Evidence," *Journal of Experimental Psychology: General*, vol. 105, 1976, pp 3-46.

Figure 1.5. Having empathy for another person's position

Involving Users Helps You to Perfect Your Product

So how do these reality checks come about? Well, considering how your users will deal with what you're creating and exposing a project to feedback early and often throughout the design process is a good start. No matter how well you think you know the mindset of those that will eventually use a system, we must always take heed that we are not our users. Even after years of watching users in testing sessions, there is always something that surprises me, something new I learn, or something unexpected.

You need to watch your users, engage with them, and persuade them to use your designs so that you can learn how they think and behave. It enables you to know them a little better, and understand the context under which they're using your product.

Some of the design projects I've worked on have required me to go into users' homes or workplaces to gain a sense of how they live and work. This has helped me to empathize with contexts of use I may be unfamiliar with, such as designing health-related devices for the elderly or chronically ill, or understanding how specialist workers do their job. Seeing users interact with initial design concepts helps to evolve our design thinking and improve our output.

Considering how to involve users in your design process can be a daunting process. Throughout this book, I'll point out situations where you can consider users' input, and offer advice on techniques at different stages of the UX process.

I'll provide practical ways to gather feedback rather than focus on lengthy engagement models. As is often cited in the UX field, some user engagement is better than no user engagement.[3] Figure 1.6 shows user engagement in action.

Figure 1.6. Context is everything

Involving the user in the design process is the best way to double-check that your approach is solving the design issue at hand. It can be tricky to deliver a great ex-

---

[3] For a commonsense approach to user testing websites, read Steve Krug's great book, *Don't Make Me Think: A Commonsense Approach to Web Usability* (Berkeley: New Riders, 2009), http://www.peachpit.com/store/product.aspx?isbn=032166860X.

perience—but all the best experiences are well thought out and pre-engineered; they don't just happen by accident.

Good and Bad User Experiences

So what are the best and worst experiences you've ever had? I'll bet that more comes to mind about an actual company or situation than just one narrow aspect of the experience itself. Personally, the best experience I've ever had was an iced coffee, like the one in Figure 1.7. Okay, that sounds ordinary on its own, but let me explain.

I was in Hong Kong on a business trip and I ordered an iced coffee in the hotel lobby. The iced coffee came out and I noticed there was ice in it. Groan. Lovers of iced coffee will know there is a fine balance between milk and coffee; putting ice in it waters down the coffee. However, when I investigated the ice cubes closely, I noticed they were made of coffee! A smart person had taken into account the problem of ice cubes watering down the coffee. This had been overcome by making ice cubes out of actual coffee, so that when they melted, the "user" was left with an equally strong coffee flavor. Brilliant!

Figure 1.7. Iced coffee anyone?

I think this illustrates beautifully what UX is all about and why it matters. My impressions of the drink and the hotel overall were elevated; I'll try to stay at that hotel every time I'm in Hong Kong now. UX takes a broad view of how a product, service, or system will work, and how it will be used by people out there in the real world. It covers the way people feel about an experience, and how satisfied they are when using it. It is often unexpected factors that have the biggest impact. This is important when solving design problems: people notice small details.

So that's the good experience; what about the bad? Well, my worst user experience involved a cheap plastic watch that I bought while my regular watch is being repaired. My life is run by the clock, and the thought of being without a wristwatch for four whole months was not an option I was going to entertain. Sure, it's the twenty-first century, and like everyone else I have a phone that displays the time and is always in reach. I just like glancing at my wrist to find out the time!

This well-known brand makes plastic Swiss watches that are cheap, fun, and loud in design; however, it was only after buying the watch I realized it was going to prove frustrating in one critical way: its inability to show the time clearly, as Figure 1.8 illustrates.

Figure 1.8. Time to buy a new watch

Showing the time is the central reason a watch exists. It seems the design team for this particular watch forgot some really basic factors; namely, to ensure the hour, minute, and second hands can be easily distinguished. Maybe there was a legitimate reason this oversight occurred, but, ultimately, as the user of the watch, I don't care much about any behind-the-scenes motivations. All I know is that I have trouble telling the time on it, and as a result I'll never buy another watch like this again.

Interestingly, my usual behavior of looking at my wrist when I need to know the time has changed with the passing of the months. Now I'm more likely to check my phone, or my computer if I happen to be sitting at my desk. As a result, I am losing the reliance I once had on my watch. This demonstrates how design has influenced my overall experience to such a degree that it has changed my behavior. We'll discuss this point more in the section called "Fogg Behavior Model" in Chapter 4.

It also illustrates what to be on the lookout for in design research. Shortcuts and workarounds that users might take tell us there's an element they're encountering that needs to be examined. This is avoidance behavior. We should home in on these alerts, as they provide hints to help us refashion a product, service, or system.

Another point to consider is the balance between utility and aesthetics. Both factors are important, but, in the end, if some item looks cool but is fairly useless, your users will soon lose interest. In my case, the watch sure is pretty, but my old one will be back in a month—at which point this watch will be retired to my daughter's jewelry box. She's three years old, so being unable to read the time won't bother her too much just yet!

I trust these examples show that we should be concerned with the opinions of our end-users. Experiences create memories for people, and there is a benefit in creating positive experiences and memories for your customers as opposed to negative ones. At the heart of it, negative experiences cost money, as angry customers are more likely to adopt another brand. Customers who are happy to refer your brand to others and speak positively about the experiences they have had with it should be your goal. In what is becoming a more and more competitive landscape, the thoughts, feelings, impressions, and experiences of users count.

Impacts on Customer Loyalty

Research has shown that companies which ensure that certain tasks require minimal effort from the customer are more likely to see greater customer loyalty.[4] Simplifying the interactions that users have with your company (or your client's company) has clear positive benefits for the bottom line. Customers that move from one brand to another cost companies money; it is easier to try to please a difficult customer than find a new one in a competitive market.

So, how easy is it to do business with your company/client's company? You need to ask yourself this when looking at the overall UX of the products you're designing.

What makes a great experience?

When creating an experience for your users, think about what might make their lives that little bit easier, saving them time and effort. If you start by defining the experience you want your users to have with your product, the rest will follow. Why? Because happy users are loyal users; it's that simple.

Great experiences differ for everyone, and there is often much banter about whether you can engineer an experience at all. What we do know is that as designers, we can manipulate a situation through our craft, because our designs can influence a user's behavior.

Your users will teach you ... so pay attention! Listen. Observe. Notice. They are revealing to you what makes a great user experience for them. If you listen and adopt a UX philosophy, you will ultimately create a better experience for everyone.

Experience of a Lifetime

In this chapter, I've introduced the idea of user experience and examined what makes a good or bad experience. I've explained what it means to focus on the UX of a product, service, or system, and how your designs will benefit by adopting this approach. In Chapter 2, we'll begin a more detailed journey into the UX process we have outlined in this chapter, taking a closer look at the research phase. Research

---

[4] Dixon, M., Ponomareff, L., and Milgramm, A., "Stop Trying to Delight your Customers: The Idea in Practice" (2012) in the *Harvard Business Review* blog [http://blogs.hbr.org/cs/2012/01/stop_trying_to_delight_your_cu.html].

will be split into two chapters: understanding the business problem in Chapter 2 and understanding the user context in Chapter 3.

Recap of What You Need to Know

▓ UX is the sum of a series of interactions a person has with a product, service, or organization.

▓ UX follows a UCD method, utilizing a range of its techniques, including being human-focused and prototype-driven as a way to understand and explore a problem.

▓ UX is a balanced approach to solving problems that starts with desirability (what does the user want or need?), balanced with feasibility (can it be done?), and viability (does it make business sense?).

▓ UX takes a multidisciplinary approach (design, HCI, industrial design, psychology, anthropology, software engineering, graphic design, and so on) and brings multiple perspectives to bear on problem-solving.

▓ UX is an approach to design and development that focuses on the context of use for the solution being designed and on having empathy for the end-users of a product, service, or system in order to improve the quality of the final solution.

Understand the Business Problem

In Chapter 1, we saw how a user experience can cover several contexts. Designing a usable digital experience for all these contexts means solving a range of problems, but it's impossible to solve a problem unless you understand it first.

The problems you encounter may appear easy to solve at first, but can quite often take many minds working together, making mistakes and then redefining the issues at hand, and challenging initial decisions to design a product that really stands out. It is important in any project to first consider the problem at hand and then explore the ways it can be approached before you get bogged down in technological development of a product.

Why do this first? Because if you resort to the computer too soon, it's easy to be caught up in grids, colors, and fonts, the organization of files, or trying to perfect layout—and forget the design problem that is before you. As tempting as it might be, avoid getting ahead of yourself. In this chapter, we'll focus on understanding the business context and target segment, and thinking about the design problem.

Research Phase

In the section called "You've Got to Have a Method" in Chapter 1, we presented a UX framework that you can follow across your projects. In this chapter, we'll focus on the first segment: the **research phase**. In this phase, you start by understanding the business context and gaining an appreciation for the key target market for your product or service, based on initial discussions with your client and other relevant areas of the business.

We'll address user research (seen in Figure 2.1) shortly. For now, we will look at understanding the business you're working with, wrapping your head around the problem before you, and structuring an approach for delivering your project. At this stage it's about setting a way forward, so that the next phases are well informed by the activities we've completed here.

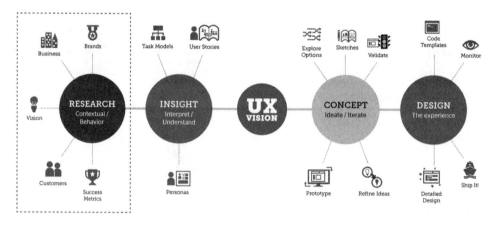

Figure 2.1. Start out by researching the business context

The Business Context

It's vital that you gain a clear understanding of your client's total business, rather than just the part that you might be working on. Your project fits within a wider business landscape, so having this context will help you comprehend your client's total value proposition. You can then identify additional areas where you can provide value.

In Chapter 1, we learned that a successful design process is led by user needs (what do people want or need?), balanced by overall feasibility (can we do it?) and viability (does it make business sense?). Having an overview of your client's entire business from the start of a project helps you to determine if what your client is asking for can actually be delivered, and whether it would make sense for them to do so.

The most successful product design understands the balance between user, business, and technical needs. With this in mind, you'll need to be exposed to other products and services across the organization before you begin your design work.

Collaborate and Communicate with Other Stakeholders

Ask your client to provide an outline of the organizational structure, and highlight the people who'll be involved with your project. Knowing these people and their perspective will be essential for you to move on your ideas and communicate your UX design approach.

Critical to your project's success is that you share the same vision for the users and their needs. Therefore, it's useful to involve your client and other company stakeholders throughout the duration of your design process. The earlier you are sharing concepts, the better. Clear communication sets the scene for solid relationships and helps to avoid the pitfalls of business politics that can often be a standard part of project work.

People who are not personally invested in the project from across the business can also help you to identify problems or issues that you need to be aware of. That means talking across departments and disciplines as a way to assure a better outcome is realized.

A Framework

Understanding your client's business means investigating areas such as:

- total business offering
- customer relationships
- business infrastructure
- revenue streams
- cost structures

This may appear to be information that's more relevant for project or business managers to extract; however, as a UX designer you'll wear several hats, and having these client discussions allows you to clarify the project's goals, particularly within a wider business context.

Figure 2.2 shows a worksheet that I find handy for guiding the discussion with the client at kick-off meetings

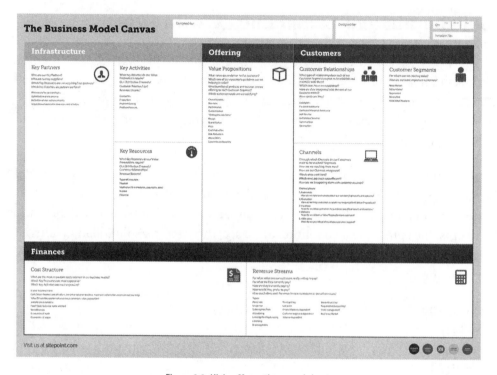

Figure 2.2. Kick-off meetings worksheet

This worksheet is based around the **Business Model Canvas** framework, a template for developing business models that investigates everything from an organization's infrastructure to its finance and customer base.[1] It helps you to engage your client and direct discussion around their business to identify its core aims, strengths, weaknesses, and priorities.

This version of the poster is available within the tools section of the book: **chapter02/business-model-canvas-poster.pdf**. Print it out and put it on a wall or large

---

[1] http://www.businessmodelgeneration.com/

table, and engage your client in the activity. Take along some sticky notes and pens, and allow the ideas you discuss to be moved around and changed as the conversation evolves.

The framework will assist you in understanding why the project is important to the company and help you to determine how your client will measure project success. From this you'll be in a better position to decide the most appropriate methods to use at various stages across the project.

Let's explore the different areas of the framework in detail.

Business Offering

Asking questions about the client's business will reveal the products and services that provide value for their customers—value that ultimately distinguishes them from their competitors. The following questions will help you to appreciate the client's business in more detail:

- What are the client's main products and services?

- What customer problems does the product or service help to solve?

- What products and services are offered to which customer segments?

- Who are the client's main competitors?

- How does the client create value to distinguish themselves from competitors?

- What customer needs are being satisfied by the client's product or services?

- Why does the client's products and services matter to customers?

- What benefits do the client's products or services create for customers?

Customer Relationships

There's bound to be a range of customer groups or segments that your client targets; however, it is vital to understand what products are geared toward which customer segments, and why. The following questions will assist you in recognizing the client's customer relationships as they see them:

- What are the key customer segments the client hopes to serve?

- What channels does the client's organization use to reach its customers?

- Which of these channels work best?

- Which channels are the most cost-effective?

- How do the channels integrate with a customer's daily routines or habits?

- What type of relationship does each segment hope to have with the client's business?

- Who are the most important customers to the client? Why?

Business Infrastructure

Gaining answers to questions about the client's business infrastructure will give you a better perspective of their product and services, and the most important activities, resources, and partners that are involved in delivering these. The following questions will help you comprehend the client's business infrastructure in more detail:

- What are the key activities that generate revenue for your client?

- What resources (human, financial, physical, intellectual) are essential for creating value for the customer?

- Who are your client's key partners or suppliers that help them to deliver products and services to their customers?

- What key activities do these partners or suppliers perform?

Revenue Streams

It is necessary to consider the financial drivers of your client's business. Are they driven by a focus on creating low-cost and no-frills products, or is their goal to create a premium product? Knowing these drivers will affect your design work, as does knowing the client's main source of revenue. The following questions will help you to distinguish the client's revenue streams:

- How does the client make money from customers?

- How does the client make money from partners?

- How do customers currently pay?

- What do customers pay for?

- How much does each channel contribute to overall revenue for the client?

- What is the total value customers are willing to pay for the product?

Cost Structures

Depending on the size and type of business, it's often useful to understand a little more about the overall cost structures involved in running your client's business. This may partly be why they've called on your talents—to help them lower the overall business costs—so it is useful to consider this up front, as it will invariably impact the way you approach your design work. The following questions will help you to identify the client's cost structures:

- What are the most important costs to the business?

- Which resources are the most expensive?

- Which activities are the most expensive?

- Is the client looking to cut costs through the use of technology? If so, how?

Why does this project matter to the client?

Now that you have a clear grasp of the overall business context, it's handy to formulate your client-focused questions around the question of *why* you have been hired to do this project. As I mentioned earlier, it is critical to identify your client's goals and objectives.

It's vital to understand how your project fits into a company strategy or how it complements other projects or business initiatives, as it helps establish who else you need to talk to within the organization.

The following questions will help uncover your client's goals and objectives for the project:

- Why is this project important to the business? Why was it initiated?

- How will the success of the project be measured internally?

- Who will be involved in determining the overall success of the project?

- Who is paying for the project (often referred to as the "project sponsor" if you're working within a larger corporate setting), and how will they be involved?

- What other areas of the business should be invited to participate in your process?

- Who will manage the expectations and involvement of other key stakeholders? (You? Your client?)

- Are there dates, time frames, or other projects that your work needs to tie into?

- Are there internal processes or constraints that you'll need to be mindful of, or work within?

It's important that you document what's discussed when you're initially engaged, listing all the objectives of the project, so that you and the client can agree on what can be achieved in the time frame.

Record the information you have collected during discussions back into your worksheet, and distribute it to your client as a clear reminder of what's been agreed upon. Your project will quite often change as it progresses; new information could come to hand, or organizational goals may shift. Having a formal record of what the original brief stated is critical.

Once you have that broader understanding of the business, it's time to start talking in more detail to your client about the users of your product.

Understand the Target Segment

Central to a UX philosophy is that the best-designed products result from understanding the needs of the people who will use them. You've already established who your client's customers are; now it's time to think about who will use the product you are designing, and how they will use it.

You should consider up front if what you're designing will take users too far from their standard routine. It's generally harder to motivate people to perform tasks that take some effort, while anything that makes life easier tends to be more successful. We'll come back to why this is the case in Chapter 4.

Your client may have a clear idea of to whom they're targeting their product. Sometimes when the product is new to market, the delineation between who is and isn't a potential user is less clear than it is for pre-existing products.

As a guide, you should focus your discussion around the following points:

- Who are the assumed users of the client's product?

- Why are these users being targeted for this product?

- What are the most critical tasks users need to complete in using the product?

- How do users currently perform these tasks (without the use of technology)?

- What behaviors are we hoping to shift or change in our customers with the product we're creating?

- What would trigger the users to want to engage with the product?

- What does the entire experience around the product and its use entail?

- How would the client define a great experience for the users of this product? Why?

- How does this experience fit with the other products and services the client has on offer?

This all comes back to gaining an appreciation for the eventual context of use for the product; importantly, it also makes you think in more detail about human behavior in relation to your product.

Understanding Human Behavior

When designing solutions for people, you need to shift your thinking toward understanding human behavior. As a designer, you already have an innate curiosity about the world around you. In creating technology for a user, this curiosity needs to be channeled into focusing on people and how they behave.

Why? Because your designs are going to influence people's behavior. This is a powerful asset, but we may not think about it when we're deeply involved in a project. You might as well direct people to where you want them to go up front, rather than just create your project and hope for the best.

So what do I mean by **behavior**? Behavior is what we do in response to the events that are happening around us daily. It is what drives our action or inaction, and dictates what we buy, eat, and think.

Going hand in hand with behavior is **habit**. Habits are a series of behaviors that lead us to act in a seemingly involuntary way. These days, many successful designers are mindful that the interfaces they design can change behavior, and this reflective process forces you to ask: what is the behavior I want to see? What outcome am I trying to design for? The digital world is a clever arena for enticing us toward new habits—some good, some bad.

Technology as a Tool to Change Behavior

New technologies, such as smartphones and tablets, have given us fast and convenient access to information. This has provided a new means for problem-solving issues in one's daily life while increasing users' level of engagement with technology. For instance, the release of exercise- or health-related apps on smartphones have assisted users in becoming more aware of their health. People can track distances ran and map their routes, count calories eaten and burned, and log their diet and sleep patterns. Similarly, money and budgeting apps have given users greater control of tracking their finances, not to mention the convenience of mobile banking.

These advances in technological interaction have influenced user behavior and habits. Good designers know what persuades us to return to their websites, whether we're habitually checking our friends' Facebook status updates, telling the world when we are asleep or awake via Path,[2] or drawn to a great news blog. As a consequence, these sites and applications can become firmly embedded in our daily lives. Before we know it, we're hooked.

Companies are collecting more data about our behavior than ever before, usually in order to target us with more of what we seem to want. Sometimes the behaviors that result from increased connectivity are adverse, such as the rise in problem gambling due to the convenience of online betting.[3]

There are times when it seems as though our brains are being rewired in new and often unexpected ways.

Other behaviors are more positive, such as the knowledge we gain by regularly interacting with mobile apps, and being able to have access to knowledge wherever we are. There are boundless opportunities right now in this time of digital revolution, targeting users with information and creating products that truly make a difference. All these developments start with thinking about what makes people tick. Design is more than just fonts and gradients, wireframes, or canvases. It is about clarifying the purpose of your product and how you want people to interact with it; then thinking about how you can shape the UX design around this. Considering why your product will matter to people and what comprises the human interaction and experience with that product holds the key to new opportunities.

A New Focus for Designers

When you think of technology as an agent for shifting or manipulating human behavior, there are golden opportunities to be had; however, part of the challenge designers and developers face is understanding what actually influences users to change their behavior in the first place.[4] As a UX researcher, I focus on what people do and why they do it in order to design better products, services, and systems that make their lives a bit easier. What we need to be mindful of when designing for

---

[2] https://path.com/

[3] For example, this article discusses the problem in Australia:
http://www.broadbandexpert.com.au/broadband-news/broadband-news/concerns-increase-over-rising-online-betting_775004

[4] Fogg, B.J. *Persuasive Technology: Using Computers to Change what we Think and Do* (San Francisco: Morgan Kaufmann, 2003)

behavior change is focusing on *how* we want people to behave with what we create.[5] Consider this statement, allegedly from the mind of Henry Ford: "If I had asked my customers what they wanted, they would have said a faster horse."

I love this quote, because it cuts to the core of the issue. As designers, we should never assume that people can project beyond their current experience to meet a future need. That's the designer's job. We can (and should) use research that employs user feedback as a tool to help us solve problems and gain an alternative perspective. We should consider the end-state behavior we hope to observe, before we even think of talking to people.

What behaviors are you hoping to change?

Thinking about behavioral goals before and throughout your research and design project is a good way to check your approach and reframe any issues you face. Goals should be revisited at intervals to remind you of where you initially set out to go; you can then test if your assumptions are working (more about that later, when we talk about prototyping and testing your designs). Focusing on user tasks and behavioral goals lessens the likelihood of being bogged down in discussions around technical features and functions at an early stage.

 Know Your ABC

The ABC of behavior model, depicted in Figure 2.3, deconstructs why an individual might behave the way they do. It works like this:

1. An event happens to trigger a behavior (*antecedent*).
2. It then causes or influences an individual to act a certain way (*behavior*).
3. This leads to the outcome you observe (*consequence*).

---

[5] Lockton, D., Harrison, D., Holley, T., & Stanton, N. A. *Influencing Interaction: Development of the Design with Intent Method*, Proceedings of PERSUASIVE 2009: Fourth International Conference on Persuasive Technology, Claremont, California, April 27-29, 2009, ACM Digital Library, New York

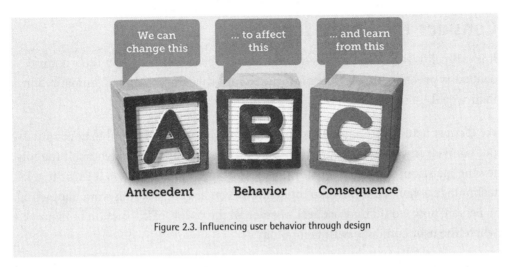

Figure 2.3. Influencing user behavior through design

Throughout our lives, most of us have been told at some point that it's impossible to change a person, but I beg to differ! What this model shows is that we can *influence the way individuals behave* by shaping the environment they function within.

When we first started talking about the type of questions to put to your client about their users, we asked ourselves: what behaviors are we hoping to change in our customers with the product we're creating? Let's now consider this in tandem with the ABC of behavior model. Focus your questions around these points, using them as part of your project kick-off template:

- How do users perform the tasks we're asking of them right now? (behavior)

- What happens to trigger a user to act in a certain way? (antecedent)

- What is the result of this? (consequence)

- How will you trigger users to perform these tasks using your product? (changing behavior)

- What is the result of this? (new behavior ... and, ideally, habit)

Discussing behavioral goals with your client early on prompts you to consider the difficulty of catering for an expected user interaction, and whether or not it will fit with a user's current ways of doing tasks.

Consider the Entire Journey

It is critical to step into your user's shoes, and observing people in their natural context is probably the most useful way to rapidly gain insight and empathy for their world.

We'll cover actually doing this in Chapter 3, but for now, it's useful to conceptually put yourself in your user's shoes; an easy way to do this is to ask yourself the following question: What is the natural way of doing things for users if I was to take technology away? That is, if the interactions you are considering were happening in person, how would they occur? Consider all the points of interaction in Figure 2.4 where the user connects with technology.

This leads us to think about what an end-to-end experience might look like for your users, and how your product would fit into their lives. Along these lines, it is helpful to consider the conversations that would occur between people, and the actions that would be initiated, if technology was not around to facilitate the exchange or transaction.

Map Your Customer Journey

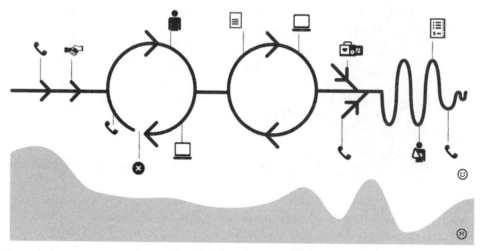

Figure 2.4. Think about the whole experience

How will your product make life easier for users?

Think about how you might move beyond a mere interface. Consider how your project fits with all your client's other products and services. Ask yourself questions about the potential user before they come into contact with your client's brand or products. What happens when they engage with the brand and product, and what about afterwards? This querying ensures that you're looking beyond the digital world, considering a broader workflow for the customer. In this sense, your thinking is moving toward the real world in which your customers live.

Points to consider:

- The beginning: where do the users come from?
- The middle: what do the users do when they arrive?
- The end: where do the users go when they're finished?

As a quick example, let's look at the experience of cooking from a recipe. Figure 2.5 depicts the context of this experience.

Figure 2.5. Cooking for an event

What this example shows is that by considering the broader user experience, you're able to think about what might make a real difference to a user when designing your product.

The Beginning

Personally, I have to have a reason to cook from a recipe—friends coming over for dinner, that sort of situation. This is what generally lifts me out of my cooking rut of standard dishes that I prepare. I'll look through my cookbooks and family recipes for inspiration, and establish what to cook based on the pictures, or how many new ingredients I have to buy. Additionally, I might skip a recipe if it seems difficult, because I want to avoid spending all night in the kitchen.

From here, I'll write a list of what I need to purchase from the shops.

The Middle

Next, I'll head to the supermarket or corner store to buy what I need, then come home and prepare for cooking. This generally entails putting the cookbook in position and reading from the recipe method. While I'm preparing the food I'll be getting the table and house ready for the guests, so a lot is going on, and I'm generally watching the clock closely.

I try to have any dishes I'm cooking up to a certain stage in the recipe so that I can get myself ready and then leave the rest until the guests arrive. This ensures that I'm still able to spend time with my friends and not be stuck in the kitchen all night, and that when we're ready to eat, the food preparation is relatively quick.

The End

Once friends have arrived, I'll spend some time sitting around, catching up and snacking on whatever I've prepared for pre-dinner nibbles. When we're ready, I'll kick things off again in the kitchen (reheating, or finishing the final steps), serve the food, and we'll eat. Figure 2.6 shows such a meal. If there are sweets, I'll clear the mains and finish off preparing the dessert, and we'll all sit around and eat, chat, and be merry. Happily, in my household whoever cooks is spared having to clean up, so my job is now done.

Figure 2.6. Ready to eat

Considering the Total Human Experience

Pondering the entire experience allows you to consider the human experience in terms of triggers, behaviors, and habits that cause the behavioral patterns you are observing. This enables you to empathize with the real social situation in which the human interaction might occur, so you can use this as a metaphor to help you shape how a human interacts with a computer.

 Using Metaphor

What do we mean by metaphor within the design context? It involves using a body of knowledge about a concept that many people are familiar with as a way to help them understand a new concept.[6]

---

[6] For more on the use of metaphor in interface design, see http://en.wikipedia.org/wiki/Interface_metaphor.

Dissecting the Workflow

Let's put this into practice with our cooking example, and imagine we're creating a recipe application. Using my dinner party metaphor, what are some lessons I might have learned by considering the entire experience from beginning to end?

- images will be a source of inspiration and will largely determine the choice of recipes

- cooking times will be a consideration dependent on the reason for cooking

- ingredients could be rated as standard (usually found in most pantries) or unusual

- difficulty ratings influence whether or not I might tackle a certain dish

- I appreciate being able to easily create a list of ingredients that I can take to the store with me

- categorizing foods as they might usually be found in a supermarket could be a time saver

- recipe steps need to be clear and simple, to avoid rereading while cooking

- for time management, steps can be divided into "tasks that can be done before guests arrive" and "tasks that can be done at the last minute"

- an audio component with reminders, recommendations, or encouragement might appeal to users; for example, "boil the water now so that the pasta will be ready on time"

- I'd like to be able to document the times the recipe was used; for instance, who I ate with, what we thought of the dish, and whether I'll do it again

- the ability to share the recipe among friends easily would be attractive

- being able to access tips and hints from friends who also cook the dish would add value

Giving yourself time to consider the broader picture helps you avoid being too solution-focused in this early stage of the project. The solution will come in time; for now, just think about the problem, and don't try to solve it.

Contemplate the Design Problem

I always find it useful to just stop and think. Then I write down what factors need more consideration at this stage, as well as what may arise throughout the remainder of the project. Why do I do this? Because it's so easy to listen to a great swathe of information and then forget some of the really important stuff.

Sometimes this turns into a log of issues and ideas, but it can be informal. The point is to record handy information while it is fresh in your mind for later reference. A simple spreadsheet will suffice, but make yourself update this periodically and refer to it.

With a fresh approach, you're able to maintain perspective about the way you felt when you first heard this information, so take a little time up front and throughout the project life cycle to document ideas; you can refer to these down the track. Figure 2.7 shows how stopping gives you time to choose which direction to travel in.

Figure 2.7. Enjoy the benefits of pausing to take stock

It's amazing how quickly you can forget stuff. These reinforced breaks keep you fresh and force you to keep the focus on your design problem.

What research approach will you use for the project?

You should now have enough information about your project to consider your overall approach. What processes will you put into place that will assist you in a successful project delivery? There are many factors that will influence this, including:

▤ internal time frames that you'll need to fit in with

▤ who else you'll be working with, internally and externally; the kind of team you'll put together, and the experts you'll consult

▤ the stages of the project that you'll be delivering (design, development, research, or all of it!)

▤ internal project approaches that your client wants you to follow, such as a certain project management approach

▤ the level of documentation you need to create and deliver for project reporting to a wider group (keeping everyone informed of where you're up to is important)

▤ sign-off points and who you engage with in this process

Ultimately, it is the design problem itself that dictates the methods you'll use. If you're yet to do so, creating a clear plan of attack should be foremost for you now. You can then discuss your plan with your client so that there are no surprises along the way.

What should the plan look like? What form should it take? The plan can be as detailed or as simple as you like. What's important is that it corresponds to the steps that were outlined in your proposal. An example of the format I often use is in Figure 2.8.

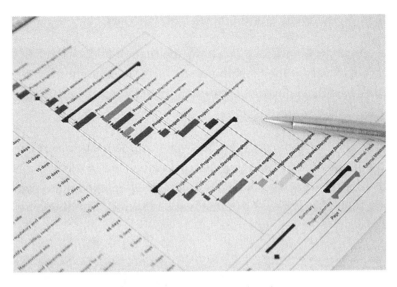

Figure 2.8. An example of a project plan

It presents activities to be completed over the course of several weeks, with key review points with the client highlighted.

The more you communicate to your client what you intend to do for them, the less confusion will occur. Time spent sharing ideas with your client, gaining feedback, and refining as needed before starting any formal activity is time well spent.

Setting a UX Project Vision

You should now have a clearer understanding of:

- the client's whole business, their customers, and their goals and objectives for the project

- who else you need to talk to within the organization for this project

- how the client's various services work together to deliver the current customer experience

- the key tasks users need to complete when using the client's product

- the customer behaviors that the client is looking to change with this product

- thinking about the big picture

▓ the type of project method and process that will work

At the start of a project, with so much new information to digest, it can be hard to determine what exactly is the most important factor to get right for your client. That's why it's useful to construct a statement that defines the experience that will be delivered.

Like design guidelines and principles, this statement helps to clarify the problem and should reinforce the reason the project was launched in the first place. One of my favorite examples of such a statement—and an often-cited one—comes from Kodak, circa 1888: "You press the button, we do the rest." It's illustrated in Figure 2.9.

Figure 2.9. A project vision can act as a guiding light

Kodak's vision here is simple, practical, and clear. It evokes a sense of shared ownership, and could easily act as a guiding light for any project team, keeping group discussions on track.

The elements of Kodak's vision that make the statement so compelling are that it:

▓ is simple to understand

▓ forgoes the detail of how an experience will be delivered

▓ takes the focus off technology

- makes complexity easier to deal with

- sets the scene for a measurement of success

- carries emotion that makes it feel like a goal worth striving for, without making false promises

- is firmly user-focused

Of course, the irony for Kodak today is that its vision, once so compelling, failed to keep pace with the rapidly changing digital landscape. "You take the picture, we do the rest" is irrelevant in a modern context; today, we as users take the picture *and also* do the rest. Even digital cameras are looking a little dated next to ubiquitous, camera-equipped smartphones, which have placed control of the total photography process firmly in the hands of the user.

What remains pertinent about the original vision is that it removes the level of complexity (technology) and focuses on the true goal: delivering a great experience to users. Inventions that appear elegant and simple have often taken many hours, several minds, and an extraordinary effort to arrive at such an advanced stage of simplicity.

Keep in mind that creating your own project vision shouldn't be an onerous task; unlike a company vision statement, no formal sign-off or approval across the organization is necessary. This point will be underscored as we discuss our upcoming case study.

What about a strategy?

In the context of a project, a vision is quite different from an experience strategy; the latter would need the collaboration and agreement of all areas of a business in order to be effectively realized. This is hard to do, so for now we'll stick to the project vision as a way of clarifying what we want to deliver at an overall experience level. We'll look at formulating an experience strategy as a reflective process in Chapter 7.

Case Study: Creating a Recipe App

I love to cook, and my love of cooking was the spark for the idea of creating a mobile app, which my company, Symplicit, will design and build to illuminate the UX process for you.

I could have picked a number of examples from the online world to showcase a UX approach; however, to my mind, nothing is quite as good as learning through a relevant and evolving case study. Although this means that the business context for the case study may not completely match the outline we have detailed above.

The Idea that Sparked the App

As I've grown older and begun cooking food for my own family, I've thought more about the food that was cooked for me as a child. I've realized that my heritage was wrapped up in the day-to-day meals I was creating and sharing with my family and close friends. Recently, I asked my mother about my grandmother's renowned baked egg custard recipe, and whether she'd written it down at all. My lovely grandmother, seen in Figure 2.10, has long since passed away, but I cherish the memory of her cooking, and feared that the recipe had perhaps passed with her, lost forever.

Figure 2.10. My grandmother, my inspiration

It's probably a common enough situation. Most of us have some dishes we remember from our childhoods that were created by different family members, but we rarely write the recipes down or share them with our family. Wouldn't it be great to have a way of recording beloved family recipes for future use, one that could be accessed easily?

So, what is the real-world problem?

If you're a keen cook like me, you might hop online to search for new additions to complement your existing collection of recipe folders and books. I rarely dig out my recipe books unless I'm in serious need of inspiration; for instance, I might just want to whip up some unique dish. My general cooking routine consists of tried-and-tested favorites I create according to a weekly cycle. These are not high-end gourmet meals, but they taste delicious!

A quick survey of friends, family, and co-workers revealed some behavioral patterns in this space. A lot of us create our own customized versions of recipes by adding little notes here and there—and then keep them stored in some form (folders, index cards, and so on). In this way, searching for and discovering recipes is a mix of digital and non-digital processes. It seems that this combination of processes could be simplified with an easy-to-use recipe app.

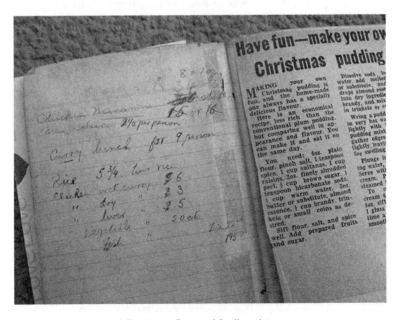

Figure 2.11. Treasured family recipes

Our first challenge is: how do we make the app compelling enough for people to use instead of their current technique, such as opening their well-thumbed recipe books? One factor in our favor is that we know many users like to create personal content, as it gives them a sense of ownership; however, creating content isn't necessarily easy—and users *like* easy.

What would convince people to record their family cooking history from scratch? What value would they gain from this? Well, the preservation of family history and the ability to share family heritage quickly and easily would definitely provide value. Imagine turning that dog-eared scrapbook brimming with recipes into a usable and impressive digital app!

Will people use the service we're creating? What will make them want to use it repeatedly? These are just some of the potential issues you'll find at the start of any process.

Is there an opportunity?

How does following a UX process help? First of all, it should settle that uneasy feeling you might have about whether or not the project will work out. To minimize any uncertainty, we have to follow a well-planned process we can trust. We need to explore the context of the real-world problem in more detail and not assume we have all the answers—after all, a quick poll among friends, family, and colleagues is hardly enough to justify an initiative of this scale.

Having the opportunity to test out assumptions by observing what real users do in relation to our design problem is going to be the easiest and quickest way to confirm or refute our assumptions.

Starting Our Plan

To begin matters, we need to set a few tasks that give us structure and a clear way forward. The plan at this stage might be as follows:

- consider the problem space (done)

- set a team in place and brainstorm the opportunity

- think about who our users might be and narrow down a key target market

- consider the behaviors we want to change in customers

- identify key questions that we need to be mindful of throughout the design process

- set a project vision, and make sure we refer to it if we question ourselves

Putting a Team in Place

In Chapter 1, we learned that part of a successful UX philosophy involves bringing several disciplines together in order to better solve design problems. In my experience, it is never useful trying to be everything to everyone; focus on what you are good at, but collaborate with other people with different skill sets when it comes to other aspects of the project.

If you work as a sole proprietor, assembling a team of experts to work with across projects can be difficult. In this case, look to your client and the talent they have in their team to assist you. Even better, consider forming a relationship with a collection of people whose work you admire or respect. One point is for sure: a group of clever people can make an idea come to life far more effectively than a single genius working solely ever could.

For our design project, we'll be doing just this: assembling a team of talented figures who will help perfect our recipe app. What sort of people will we need?

- a *researcher*, so that we can engage with our users, conduct contextual investigation, and refine and iterate our design ideas through user-based testing

- *designers* from the spheres of visual, typographic, and industrial design who will bring creative knowledge to the issue at hand

- an *interaction designer* to help us think about the interactions across pages, as well as the overall continuous flow of the entire experience

- a *developer* who would work with us to rapidly prototype the app and test ideas on the fly

There we are in the Figure 2.12; there are only seven of us. We have a mix of research, design, strategy, and development capabilities.

Figure 2.12. Meet the team

Ten Questions to Kick Off this Project

 What's on your mind?

What are you thinking about in relation to creating the recipe app right now? What are the questions you might put to the client? Take a minute to write down ten items that you require more information on before continuing.

All done? I'm sure you were able to come up with a few queries at this point in the proceedings, but if you were shy of ten, here are some questions for you to ponder:

- How do people currently store and share their recipe information?

- What would encourage people to start using a digital format instead of their hard-copy version?

- Would people input recipes they already have in hard copy?

- We believe this app will be highly personal as it represents the preservation of family history, but is that how others will see it?

- Would people want to share recipes via a social network?

- How do people categorize recipe information?

- Are there any similar applications that already exist?

- What kind of designs and branding will we use?

- Will we aim for a smartphone platform, a tablet, or both?

- What operating system will we focus on: iOS, Android, Windows 7, or as many as possible?

Behavioral Change

One aspect of this project will involve fundamentally changing the way people record and store recipe information; we are talking about a major shift in behavior.

At a basic level, we want people to start using the app, so this is the first behavior to encourage. Ideally, we want recipe creation in our app to be a habit. This means that whenever users even think about documenting or sharing recipes, they put it in the app. These are the basics we need to consider.

What are some of the other behaviors we'd like to shift our users toward? We could encourage them to:

- create and store recipes digitally

- abandon paper and pen formats, but tie in an offline component; for example, make pages printable for a cookbook

- share recipes with others digitally

- invite family and friends to this space

- document everyday recipes, instead of just occasional gourmet meals

- check the app regularly and engage in dialogue with other users

■ feel *compelled* to document all their culinary experiences here

Further behavioral shifts might emerge as our project progresses; but for now, these goals are enough.

A Project Vision

The impetus for creating this app was the knowledge that some of my grandmother's recipes might be lost forever if a family member had not remembered to keep them safe. In a way, the app will form a piece of personal history for users rather than being just a document of favorite recipes. So the main focus of the project will be how it provides a way for users to share and record their family heritage using recipes.

In this respect, working in the digital arena allows us to record family history using dynamic methods that provide some extra oomph; for instance, we can incorporate videos with various recipes. Family and friend connections gain a more hands-on dimension.

Another focal point is to make the app incredibly easy to use, otherwise nobody's going to even try to use it. Not only do the design and interactions need to be simple, we must avoid placing too great a load on our users in creating content for their digital recipe book. If it's too much of an effort to create content, why would a user bother to move to a whole new process?

 The Vision Splendid

Before we continue, let's think about our app's project vision. Recall the elements that are most important: it should focus on the user, it needs to be simple, and it must remove technology from the picture. What would your project vision be? Take a minute to think about your project vision, write it down, and then we'll compare notes.

Here's the vision statement I came up with for the recipe app:

Sharing the food we love from the past and present with the people we are closest to, and making it stupidly simple to do so.

Got one of your own?

How does this statement compare to the one you arrived at? What are the differences?

This vision statement describes what will be the app's unique aspects, because it:

- has personal and emotional aspects

- will document recipes from our day-to-day lives, rather than recipes we've found on the Web

- should represent home cooking and simple food (nothing too fancy!)

- has to be shared with friends

- must be easy to use

The Bottom Line

Recap of What You Need to Know

- Talk to your client and study their business from a broader perspective, covering areas such as their:

    - business offering
    - customer relationships
    - business infrastructure
    - revenue streams
    - cost structures

- Collaborate and communicate with other stakeholders.

- Balance business needs (is it feasible and viable?) with user needs (will people want this product?).

- Understand the end-to-end service customers currently experience with the business.

- Think about the human context:

- Who are your users?
- What are their key tasks?
- What will define a great experience?

- Know which behaviors you're targeting for change.

- Make a plan for your project and consider what you should be mindful of at this point.

- Set a clear project vision and refer to it constantly; this statement will help you and your stakeholders navigate through the project and make clearer decisions.

In Chapter 3, we'll learn some excellent UX methods for engaging users with our app by examining how people are interacting with technology. We'll then incorporate this into our project context. Let's get stuck in!

Understand the User Context

In Chapter 2, we looked at the necessity of understanding the business problem you've been asked to solve, as well as its business context. This process included gaining an appreciation of the target market for your product or service.

In this chapter, we'll keep our focus on the research phase of our UX process, but we'll be looking at the user context. We'll investigate methods that are useful for engaging users at this stage of your project.

Keep in mind that we'll be interacting with our users several times throughout each phase of the UX framework, as well as during the concept stage and the design stage (more on these in Chapter 5). My aim is to steer you towards the right methods for the design problem you face. Remember, we're still in the research phase of the UX process, as indicated in Figure 3.1.

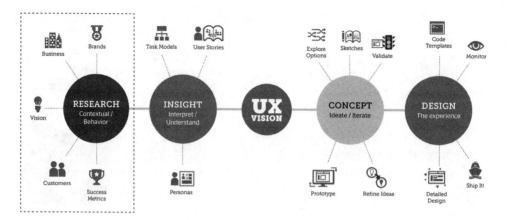

Figure 3.1. Investigating the user context in the research phase

In this chapter, we'll discuss entering the user's world to understand it, choosing user experience research methods, and identifying and recruiting users.

Moving into the User's World

Good designers understand how to solve problems and create elegant solutions, but also know the value of considering other perspectives when doing so. Expertise within a given profession is often a combination of intuition, experience, some guesswork, and perhaps a touch of magic. Given the gulf between experience and more random factors, it's necessary to move into your user's world to gain a sense of how they live and work.

You'll also need some level of user research in your design projects.

Users Aren't Designers

It's unrealistic to think, however, that asking a bunch of people about your design problems will yield a complete solution.

If you're a fan of *The Simpsons*, you may remember "The Homer" car. This is the episode where Homer's half-brother Herb gives him a job at Powell Motors. Despite complaints from his staff, Herb encourages Homer to follow his instincts and create a car that average American consumers would want to buy. The outcome? Disastrous … and hysterical![1]

As well as being strange, Homer's creation cost so much to develop and had such a high price tag that Herb's company went out of business. In effect, Homer created a car that came out of his current life experience. This approach clearly failed to follow the rules of balance covered in Chapter 1 and Chapter 2, whereby you should always account for desirability (human requirement) against viability (business requirement) and feasibility (technology requirement). Never expect people to look beyond their current experience in order to come up with a great solution for you. That's your job.

If we let our users make all the decisions (desirability without viability or feasibility), we'd end up with a horse designed by committee, as shown in Figure 3.2.[2]

Figure 3.2. Never ask your users to design—you might not like the result

---

[1] Check out the Simpson's Wiki [http://simpsons.wikia.com/wiki/The_Homer] for an image of the actual car.
[2] http://en.wikipedia.org/wiki/Design_by_committee

Combining Methods for Best Effect

The most successful UX research projects involve participants who think carefully about the questions presented, enabling you to creatively plan a mix of methods that aid your design ideas. You should try to use at least two or three methods across a project life cycle, as illustrated in Figure 3.3. You can then review the results obtained across methods and observe themes, overlaps, or contradictions, as well as prevent misleading findings. It also allows you to determine the strongest insights from each method, resulting in a far richer understanding of your users.

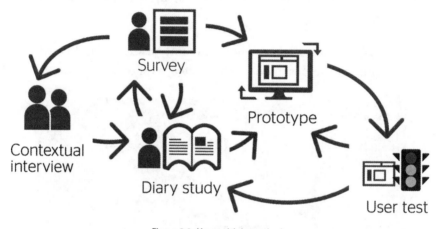

Figure 3.3. Use multiple methods

 A Blast from the Past

What process did you use on your last project? Did you engage users in your design efforts, and if so, how? What was the project's outcome? What worked well, and what do you wish you had done differently? How will you engage users in your next project?

Choosing Your UX Method

It's important to have a clear plan *before* you approach your users. Research is good for helping you with problem-solving and design work; however, research without a focus is merely guesswork.

Formulate Your Questions

Remember our ten-questions activity in the section called "Putting a Team in Place" in Chapter 2? Use these initial questions to structure what you want to talk to users about. No doubt you've expanded upon this list with a few what-ifs. Make sure you add these to the mix.

So how do you know if the questions asked are the right ones? There's a technique to help you here, known as The 5 Whys. You can try it yourself, or as a brainstorming session with others.

Ask Why—and Then Ask It Again

The 5 Whys technique helps you to decide if your questions are related to a real problem or not, and shows you how to map the relationship between root causes of a problem. The benefit of the 5 Whys is that no formal statistical analysis is required. The process simply consists of looking at your problem and asking a series of incremental "why?" questions (normally five, but of course you can ask more depending on the situation).

Let's take a look at it, using the recipe app as an example. Specifically, let's say the user wants to be able to locate and preserve recipes from family members:

1. Why?

   Otherwise they'll be lost forever.

2. Why does this matter?

   Because some of the recipes I loved as a kid have been lost over the years.

3. Why does this matter?

   Because it is like losing a little piece of your family's history.

4. Why does this matter?

   Because I love to cook and want to pass on the recipes I cook to my family when they grow up and leave home, so that they have a record of the food we ate and shared together.

5. Why?

Because it would be great to have a permanent personal record of recipes and family photos of us enjoying the food we shared together. Future generations could see it, and could share and enjoy the food we cooked.

You can use the 5 Whys to analyse users' comments when conducting research in general, as well as up front to narrow down your core research questions. Start broad and aim for quantity; then use the 5 Whys to explore your questions more deeply, helping you to decide which are most relevant to your research efforts.

This is also a useful activity to undertake with your client to check their core questions and assumptions, as well as other team members. Once you've determined the core questions to explore with users, you can choose the type of UX research methods applicable to your project.

Preparing for Research

Here's what you'll need to address when involving users in UX research:

- Plan the method you'll follow to keep users engaged and responsive.

- Create a list of tasks you'll use to interact with users, such as prompts for contextual inquiry, scenarios to walk through when doing user-based testing, design problems to set up in design workshops, and so on. We'll cover what these are shortly.

- Screen the participants against predefined criteria; this enables you to filter who you select against your particular needs. Look at incentives for the participants, such as cash payments, movie tickets, gift cards, or free food.

- Prepare to interact with participants by establishing the meeting space; think about scheduling visits to your users at their workplace or home. Consider whether you'll hire a lab for user-based testing, or set up in your client's office or your own.

- Work out how you'll capture the information you observe—for example, notes or video footage—and how you'll analyze your data.

- Finally, recruit your users (we'll go into detail on how to do this in the section called "The User Interview", so hold this thought).

I like to keep in touch with some of the users engaged in up-front contextual research, and invite them back throughout the design process for workshops and testing sessions. This way they can comment on changes made as the design evolves. This approach helps balance feedback between those who've had no exposure to the product, and those who have been part of the entire research journey.

Method Types

As I mentioned in Chapter 1, UX methods are generally focused around observation as the data source, with conclusions being qualitative in nature. You can divide research into whether it requires direct or indirect user contact.

Table 3.1 provides a summary of the different types of user research methods you might encounter, but it's by no means exhaustive. Some of the terms might be new to you, but we'll be covering the most important ones later when we discuss some of the more common methods in detail.

Table 3.1. Different types of user research

Type of Approach	Research Method	Helps to Answer ...	How many samples needed?
Users' preferences: their opinions, likes, and desires	Questionnaire or survey (indirect) Focus group Customer feedback	What do users think about?	Larger volumes: hundreds to thousands for a survey; four to 20 for focus groups
Exploratory: investigating the context in which users complete tasks, helping to understand habits, motivators, drivers, and behaviors	Contextual inquiry Behavioral interview Diary study (indirect) Mental models	What is an individual trying to accomplish?	Smaller samples with this type of research: 12 inquiries or interviews; four to six diary studies
Summative: what is understood or accomplished with a product?	Usability tests Card sort (can be direct or indirect) Design workshop	Can users complete tasks?	Smaller samples with this type of research: eight to 12 users for testing and card sorts; four to six for workshops

Different techniques will help at different stages of the UX process, so you should always choose the method that's most appropriate for the types of questions you have to ask, as well as the needs of the project at that point. You may feel more comfortable implementing some methods over others due to their familiarity; for example, usability testing is probably better known to many of you than contextual inquiry. Still, I encourage you to try each of them, as it will help you develop sound judgment. Over time, you'll come to know which tool you should be pulling out of your research arsenal, and when best to use it.

Now I will present a few techniques that produce what I believe to be the best outcomes for this stage of the process.

The User Interview

User interviews are a valuable method for kicking off exploratory research, as mentioned in Table 3.1, although they present some areas of concern. Trusting what users *say* against what they actually *do* can be problematic. Humans are usually bad at self-reporting, and when challenged, often make up stuff on the spot. There are a range of psychological reasons for this which are beyond the scope of this book—but nonetheless, be warned.

Still, a user interview will help you practice your 5 Whys, and zero in on the problems that users raise during the course of conversation. It allows you to explore general attitudes, look deeper into motivators and drivers, and explore workflows. You can ask users to recall specific instances when they've done a task well or when it proved a challenge, and have them relay the events in detail. The more structured you make the conversation with current or potential users of your product, the better.

Figure 3.4. Interviewing your users

Some tips to help you succeed with a user interview include:

- Have users complete a pre-session homework activity (see the section called "Priming Activity"). It will help guide discussions when you're new to interviewing, as well as provide topics of conversation.

- Ideally, conduct the interview at the users' homes or workplaces, where they are "within context" of the topics you might be discussing.

- Have a plan for the results you want to gain from the interviews and put together a page of prompts so that you can focus the conversation towards achieving this.

- Pay attention to your 5 Whys and use them to assist with your questioning; encourage open conversation so as to avoid one or two-word responses (closed questioning).

- Be flexible with your structure if it means achieving the outcomes you need.

- Choose questions that probe thoughts, feelings, beliefs, reactions, and tasks that people complete, and ask "why?" liberally as a way to dig a bit deeper.

- Ask users about a time when they experienced difficulty in completing tasks, as well as a time when it all went well.

- Home in on any useful shortcuts or workarounds that users mention.

- Try to keep the interview to one hour, as attention spans wane after this time.

Contextual Inquiry

In Table 3.1, we mentioned **contextual inquiry**. This is an unstructured interview that occurs in the context in which your product or service will be used, so that you can observe and record the way people work and behave. In a contextual inquiry, you'll witness a user's common habits and working techniques, asking questions when necessary and recording your observations, which should influence your design of the product or service.

Your main job here is to learn from your users: observe how they work and question them when you need to clarify details. Contextual inquiry is often used to uncover unmet needs or hidden desires; it's also a good way to discover how people think and talk about a given topic. Remember that *how* people speak about tasks and events, including the terms they use, can often reveal hidden issues and problems waiting to be resolved through good design. Figure 3.5 shows the environment in which a contextual inquiry took place, as well as the gestures performed by the user while talking about their cooking habits.

Figure 3.5. Observe your users in the context of their everyday behavior

Some tips to help you succeed with contextual inquiry:

- Clarify what is the most important context of use (work or home) for your project.

- Consider how many interviews per day you can undertake when travel is involved to conduct these sessions. Recruit your users and schedule a time to visit them that matches an overall schedule. Ask permission if you want to record users in their natural context (usually a cash incentive is needed for this).

- Treat people with respect and avoid passing judgment on the way users perform tasks. Think of yourself as a student trying to learn what it is that the user does and how they do it. For example, if you're designing a mobile app for athletes, put on your trainers and go for a run. Feel what it might be like to be fit and healthy, and then consider what matters most to potential users about their passion for running.

- It's fine to be curious and probe for more information. Your 5 Whys are always good fallbacks for questioning.

- Learn to think on your feet and follow the natural flow of the situation; it's okay to abandon the script.

■   Remember, random tangents can provide the best insights into users' private worlds. Let them go off on these tangents—you might find gold!

Diary Studies

Diary studies, seen in Figure 3.6, were also mentioned in Table 3.1. They enable your users to document the way they work relative to a given topic area over a period of time. As the designer, you will usually create the kit for participants to record their work, and later review it with them.

Often, I'll leave an A3 workbook with a participant following an initial briefing; sometimes I might leave additional tools, such as a cell phone that they can use to take photos or text me with questions as they pop up. This is to uncover elements that the participants may have failed to reveal, or that you might have missed when conducting a contextual inquiry.

Figure 3.6. Diary studies

Here are a few tips when it comes to mastering diary studies:

■   Diary studies should be combined with a pre- and post-interview briefs to bring the participant up to speed on your expectations; in the post-interview follow-up, have the participant walk through their diary and discuss the information they have recorded.

- Contact your users regularly to discuss what they've been doing and recording, and redirect activities if necessary.

- It's useful to conduct an in-person catchup midway through the process to review what has been done.

- Any user output—such as comments or sketches, for instance—are handy to refer to in later design and development processes, as they represent a strong user voice.

Priming Activity

I've used priming activities on my projects for a while now. A **priming activity** is essentially a homework activity for research participants to complete before we meet with them. We have them create a collage of words and images on a poster-size piece of cardboard or paper that answers a broad research question concerning the topic area of interest; for example, we might ask participants to show "What cooking means to me, personally." You can see an example of this in Figure 3.7.

No matter what the research process (user-testing, contextual inquiry, and so on), I ask participants to complete this homework activity before I see them. I find this advance activity acts as a great way to kick off the session, as primed participants are more relaxed and engaged about discussing the topic of interest. Priming activities also represent a quick way to gather insights about your users when you lack the time or budget to conduct a contextual inquiry or diary study.

The origins of this method tie in design and brand research, as well as family psychology, where it allows participants to create links with information to reflect the way they think; moreover, it often uncovers aspects they might think to discuss, or are even consciously aware of. The activity taps into both left- and right-brain thinking, so the visual nature of the output is great for exploring design research. You can find the homework sheet we send to participants in the tools section of this book to download as a template (**chapter03/homework-activity-template.dotx**) and as an example (**chapter03/homework-activity-recipe-app.docx**).

Figure 3.7. Priming your users for homework

Here are a few hints to help you construct a priming activity:

- Create a guide for users to follow and send it to them to complete before you meet with them (I generally send it to users for research as soon as they've been recruited).

- Ask a broad question about the topic area. For example, "how do you feel about managing your finances?" "How do you feel about cooking and meal preparation?" Take care to avoid biasing your users' thinking, and encourage them to think in a general way.

- Have participants use an A3-sized (or larger) piece of paper or cardboard to complete the activity, and instruct them to use a mixture of images, words, and quotes about the given topic.

Usability Testing

Probably the best known of all UX methods, **usability testing** is a technique for evaluating how easy a product or service is to use by having end-users complete a set of typical tasks. It can be used in your initial research stages, as shown in Figure 3.8, to evaluate how an existing product usually performs (known as **benchmarking**), in order to shape the approach you take with your current design efforts.

Figure 3.8. Usability testing

You can have users test across a range of competing or complementary websites; any feedback may help shape your design work. What's handy about this method is that there's no need to wait until everything is fully designed before you draw on it; you're basically testing prototypes of the final system during the design evolution.

Here are a few tips to help you along the usability testing path:

■ Recruit users through lists from your client or a third-party recruiter.

■ Most usability-testing sessions employ somewhere between eight to 12 users. Large numbers are unnecessary when it comes to identifying patterns in behavior.

■ Set a clear start time when scheduling for sessions. Try to keep sessions to an hour and a half maximum.

■ Ensure you have a clear set of tasks for your users to complete, and discuss their ease or difficulty with your client up front.

■ User-based testing can be used to evaluate a product that already exists, or to evaluate a user's performance with competing products. It can also effectively test ideas early on in the design process (concept stage) and in later phases (low- or high-fidelity design stages). In this sense, it's one of the most flexible methods in UX.

■ To achieve the most from your sessions, encourage your participants to think aloud. Avoid answering direct questions from your user; instead, redirect them back to their own considerations, with guiding questions such as: "What would you expect?", "What are your thoughts on this?", or "How do you think it might be done?". We'll outline this process in greater detail in Chapter 7.[3]

■ Set a measure of a concept's success or failure. A simple five-point scale is a good way to rate the difficulty of a task. For example, 1 and 2 = fail; 3 = bench- mark performance; 4 and 5 = little or no issues noted.

Some Quick and Dirty Options

We've just covered a number of formal techniques for performing user research. There are also a handful of unconventional methods that require less effort while still yielding useful results. These methods can provide quick and effective user feedback at the start of your project—feedback that can really aid your understanding of the design problem.

I caution that these methods also need to be tested against wider audience opinion using additional techniques for validation. Nevertheless, I've personally found these approaches to be quite revealing in the early stages of a project as a quick sense- check.

 First Impressions

Take a moment to consider the research questions you've formulated. At first glance, what methods do you think will be useful for researching our users' beha- vior? Why?

---

[3] More on this in Krug (2005).

Recruiting via Social Media

There have been a number of times when I've thrown a question to a select group of people on Facebook via the **Messages** area, particularly if it's related to the design of mass-consumption products and services (or customer-focused products or services).

This is a quick way to capture the opinions of many people from different walks of life, and you're guaranteed at least a few instant responses thanks to the popularity of Facebook. Obviously, the larger your network, the more results you'll see. The people I select might have gone to school with me, or are friends of friends, or acquaintances who don't work in marketing, IT, or the corporate world. Using Facebook has become an easy way for me to gather opinion from a large cross-section of individuals locally and internationally who lack the technical chops.

In a recent example, I asked people: "What does self-service mean to you?" The responses challenged my preconceptions, and generated a healthy discussion among the group; they quickly bounced ideas off each other, and even asked for another question the next day! It was like a virtual focus group or crowdsourcing approach that I moderated from afar to keep on track. Was it useful? Definitely! Would I do it again? Absolutely.

Don't Ask Friends and Family!

In Chapter 1, I mentioned that I often ask myself, "How would my parents react to this?" as a way to sense-check my own design work. However, I'd caution against going ahead and *actually asking* your parents, close friends, or family to evaluate your design work. Why? Because they're less likely to admit if something makes no sense—in fact, they're probably going to want to protect your feelings.

You want to know when projects aren't working, so an endless stream of positive statements from well-meaning relatives will be no help on launch day if your design was actually quite poor. Useful results from user research requires the feedback of relevant users, so it's probably best to avoid pulling out your designs at the next family catch-up.

Create a Chat Group

In our office, we use an application called Yammer that allows us to chat internally, much like an internal Twitter client. Recently, I've started using Yammer's **Groups** function to invite users into a conversation when they're involved in research projects that span a long time frame. For example, I might have conducted a contextual inquiry at the homes or workplaces of these people; it would be beneficial, then, to include them in further design workshops or user-based testing sessions.

By using a chat application such as Yammer, you can create a forum that provides ready access to these users and allows you to pose questions, post design concepts, and just generally engage and interact with them. It's also effective for obtaining quick feedback from users and sharing ideas with your client.

Any contact with users is better than none. The key is to keep an open mind and continually sense-check your ideas. While the results will fall short of providing all the answers, they'll at least ensure you're keeping users at the forefront of your mind and challenging your assumptions early and often.

This leads us to the next question: how do you choose your users for research? We'll now consider how to recruit your users for UX research.

Recruiting the Right People

Choosing the right users when you conduct research is critical for an effective outcome. In order to do so, you need to apply filters that detail some specifics about the type of people you're after. If you are yet to begin research, you should consider catching up with professionals in other parts of the client's business you're consulting with to establish their take on the key target group; people who work in marketing, branding, customer support services, or product management tend to have a good handle on who typifies the target market. And if there's a department that specializes in UX as part of the business, that's obviously a great place to start!

In this section, we'll cover some user characteristics that you may recognize from client discussions, highlight the areas on which to focus your efforts, and help you narrow down who you bring into your user research. Figure 3.9 suggests that your users are under three.

Figure 3.9. Choosing the right people is critical

What does the client's business have that can help?

The organization you're working with is likely to have a range of documents to help you define your product's audience, such as:

- user or market research (that might relate to your project)
- customer segmentation models, user profiles, or personas
- site statistics or customer intelligence (such as feedback received from the website or through the call center)

UX Research Is Not Market Research

Quite often, UX research methods unearth user characteristics and needs that have not previously been documented by a business. This is because businesses often engage in market research, which is traditionally based on survey or focus group data and relies on users' self-reporting capacity. The data from market research should be considered with caution—mainly because we humans are fairly bad at verbally reporting what we do and why we do it.

UX methods focus on observing behaviors and habits as a way to expose unmet needs and design opportunities; these have no reliance on self-reporting, and produce more trustworthy sources of data. Table 3.2 outlines examples of user criteria that are most often cited within organizations.

Table 3.2. Different types of user data

Type of Data	Examples
Demographic	▪ Gender ▪ Age ▪ Income ▪ Education level
Geographic	▪ Metropolitan locations ▪ Regional locations
Psychographic	▪ Personality ▪ Values ▪ Attitudes ▪ Interests ▪ Lifestyle
Behavioral	▪ Usage rate ▪ Loyalty ▪ Task focus
Firmographic	▪ Industry ▪ Seniority ▪ Functional area

Making a List of Potential Users

Once you've collected any information about a target audience from your client, the next step is to clarify in your own mind who you think would use the product. Here are some steps to help you along this road:

1. Brainstorm with others or just think about the key tasks required of users when engaging with the product.

2. Group these tasks into categories.

3. Make up some category names; for example, in the case of our recipe app we could have Single Foodies, Family Caterers, Home Leavers, and Gourmet Grays.

4. Consider tying these category types back to some of the market research data you've encountered and compare notes.

This process helps you consider your product's user base and forces you to think about the customer differently than from standard demographics alone. Most of the recruitment specifications that I've sent to a third-party agency have a mix of behavioral characteristics and demographic data. It helps me to broadly trace the people I expect to recruit into the research process, and place them in categories my client sees as their customers. For instance, we may use demographics such as age, gender, education, or income, to name a few.

Right person for the job?

Just remember that the more specific you make your criteria, the harder it might be for your recruiter to find the right people. Still, it is important that the people you see are relevant. Make sure you give enough time to this task.

Recruiting Tools

You'll find an example recruitment specification in the tools folder that accompanies this book: **chapter03/recruitment-specification-template.dotx**. Download this template as a useful starting point.

Going Left of Center

I've always found it useful to look beyond the users seen as central to the client's target market, and consider some **edge cases**. You learn a great deal from edge cases, but what are they? In the same way we sometimes choose to say what something *isn't* rather than what it is, when we evaluate our designs we should think about extreme user-types that operate a bit differently to the norm. This uncovers new or unexpected insights and helps to clarify our product boundaries; for instance, an age range, or a certain level of proficiency.

Here's an example of using an edge case from a recent project in the financial services sector. I was researching wealthy customers, observing their financial habits and the behaviors they undertake automatically without further thought. Additionally,

I included users in my research who were struggling financially, or had fallen into bankruptcy. This helped to reveal some of the difficulties people face while trying to juggle financial management tasks in day-to-day life. These insights led to a design solution that would ultimately appeal to both ends of the financial spectrum.

You'll gain a better understanding of how to approach your design problem if you view it from both angles, as seen in Figure 3.10.

Figure 3.10. Know your main players, but live on the edge a bit, too

 Cooking on the Edge

Take a moment to consider how you'd complete this activity for the recipe app. What are the user's key tasks? Who would do them? Cook up some clear categories of users you think represent our key target market, as well as some edge cases.

Case Study: Understanding the User Context

Putting all this information in context, the steps we take for our recipe app should look like this:

▓ Clarify the questions we want to ask our users and further explore them through research (using our 5 Whys to brainstorm with our client and our team).

- Access any background demographic information on our audience segments, brainstorm who we think our users are, and create personas (user profiles).

- Decide what research methods would suit the questions we want answered.

- Prepare the materials we need and recruit the participants.

- Once recruited, go to where the app will eventually be used (in our case, the user's kitchen), and listen to what's said—and not—for an idea of the context our design will end up in.

Personas

Personas are fictional characters that are created to represent the various user types of a certain product. These characters are given names, photos, and details relevant to the task at hand, ensuring that all consumer segments of the product or brand are given a voice.

Clarifying Questions

We now want to recap and expand upon the questions documented in the section called "Ten Questions to Kick Off this Project" in Chapter 2. Some additional questions may have arisen as you read through this chapter. What were they? For me, they were:

- What type of role does cooking and recipes play in people's lives?

- How and where are cookbooks and cooking references stored?

- When do people refer to recipe books, and when do they use recipes from memory or improvise?

- How do people share recipe information? What are the current tools for doing this?

- Has anyone shared recipes with their family that they recall eating as a child? When do they cook these? Are these stored differently to other recipes?

- When people are cooking, at what points in time do they actually refer to recipe information in a book?

■ How do they read recipe instructions while cooking?

■ How do users talk about food and cooking? What is the language they use to categorize recipes?

I'm sure you can see how the questions are becoming more task-focused. This is important, as we're going into users' environments to watch them do a job: the job of cooking and meal preparation. How did your questions compare to mine?

Who are our recipe app users?

We need to brainstorm the type of people who might use our app, as well as what tasks they're likely to complete concerning food. Our food-related tasks list might look a little like Table 3.3 (keeping in mind that this is more a "brain dump" of ideas at this stage):

Table 3.3. Key tasks related to food and cooking

Cooks food	Goes out to dinner
Buys organic food	Buys food at the supermarket
Buys at local corner shops	Always eats out
Enjoys sharing food	Shares recipes
Talks about cooking	Watches food shows
Usually has nothing in the pantry	Cooks food mother made
Has dinner parties	Finds it hard to cook
Dreams of being a chef	Searches the Web for recipes
Prints out recipes to store and save	Downloads recipe apps
Cooks the same dishes most of the time	Shares photos of food
Uploads photos of food to social media	Buys takeout a lot of the time
Grows own food	Buys food magazines
Emails recipes	Cooks for fun
Lives a healthy lifestyle	Enjoys trying new food
Has secret recipes	Talks about food when in company
Stores recipes	Dislikes cooking

Clustering Tasks to Create User Types

Our next task is to:

▪ Group tasks into clusters to make the data manageable; for example, Shares recipes, Stores recipes, Cooks regular meals, and so on.

▪ For all the groups you create, ask yourself, "Who would do this?"

▪ Make up names that fit the type of people you imagine would behave in this way.

 Categorically Speaking

How would you cluster these tasks to form logical groupings? Take a minute to think this through and then we'll compare notes.

Naturally, it helps to consider your users in a task-focused manner, as this ultimately informs the type of people you'll recruit. For our recipe app, we need to come up with groups of users that fit the tasks we've outlined, such as:

▪ young children cooking

▪ kids and their friends

▪ home-leavers who can't cook (edge case)

▪ people who struggle with cooking and therefore hate it (edge case)

▪ people who've been living away from home for a while

▪ people who date regularly and like impressing others with cooking

▪ single couples that love cooking

▪ parents with kids

▪ parents with kids not living at home

▪ grandparents who entertain or eat out

▪ chefs or professional cooks and writers (edge case)

We'll now refine these groups to logical segment names, and create our recruitment brief for an agency. These will also form the basis of the user personas we construct.

Defining Our Initial Cut of Users

The initial target groups might be:

- Home leavers: social, young adults who've just left home, and food is more about sustenance than enjoyment

- Single foodies: unmarried, childless people for whom cooking and sharing food is a huge part of their lives

- Family caterers: people with youngish kids who used to love dinner parties, but whose focus is now on feeding their brood of mainly unadventurous and fussy eaters

- Gourmet grays: time-rich empty-nesters and grandparents for whom cooking means family, and whose many family events revolve around eating and meal preparation

These groupings (further illustrated in Figure 3.11) form the basis of skeleton personas that we'll refer to during our design efforts. These will be further refined in the section called "Thinking about Cooks" in Chapter 5 once we've undertaken user research.

Figure 3.11. First persona sketches for the app

The Recipe Game Plan

This plan allows us to do the research and design in parallel, so that we make best use of the time available and feed insights back into the design process as we go. Here's the plan I put together and how it looks as we move through the UX process:

Setting a Time Frame

Our time frames are determined by the:

- progression of chapters in this book and final book launch (main driver)

- time period within which we could reserve a name within the app store: 90 days (secondary driver).

Research Phase

We'll need to engage our users at various times throughout the UX process to understand the context in which they'll use our product. In the research phase, engaging users will involve the following methods:

- sending the priming activity to users for the contextual inquiry prior to meeting them, encouraging them to consider how they feel about food preparations and planning; this will then allow us to kick off conversations

- conducting a mix of contextual inquiry and at-home interview processes with four users, where we observe the participants cook a meal and ask them questions during the task of cooking

- providing one or two participants with a diary study so that they can document their cooking habits and behaviors over a two-to-three-week period

- creating a social media discussion group for participants to communicate with each other and design team members, and to enable us to put questions and even concept designs to the group as required; consider the online social network conversation about recipes in Figure 3.12 s

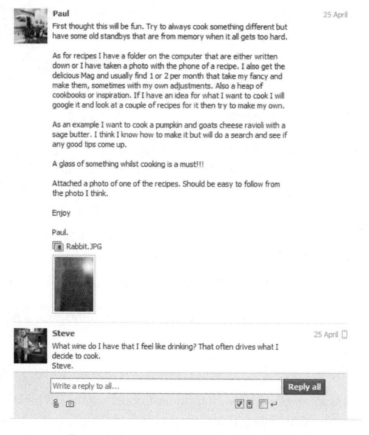

Paul   25 April

First thought this will be fun. Try to always cook something different but have some old standbys that are from memory when it all gets too hard.

As for recipes I have a folder on the computer that are either written down or I have taken a photo with the phone of a recipe. I also get the delicious Mag and usually find 1 or 2 per month that take my fancy and make them, sometimes with my own adjustments. Also a heap of cookbooks or inspiration. If I have an idea for what I want to cook I will google it and look at a couple of recipes for it then try to make my own.

As an example I want to cook a pumpkin and goats cheese ravioli with a sage butter. I think I know how to make it but will do a search and see if any good tips come up.

A glass of something whilst cooking is a must!!!

Attached a photo of one of the recipes. Should be easy to follow from the photo I think.

Enjoy

Paul.

Rabbit.JPG

Steve   25 April

What wine do I have that I feel like drinking? That often drives what I decide to cook.
Steve.

Write a reply to all...   Reply all

Figure 3.12. Some Facebook conversation around recipes

Concept Phase

In the concept phase, engaging users encompasses these techniques:

- overseeing design workshops at various intervals in the design process so that we can bounce off ideas and gain feedback on designs from initial raw sketches through to high-fidelity designs (internal activity)

- conducting small design workshops to present sketches and any wireframes to gain initial reactions, in order to help shape our thinking (user focus)

- continuing to use the social media groups as a forum to share design ideas and concepts rapidly for feedback as we progress through design cycles and refine the final design for final validation with users

- inviting some users from the previous phases and recruiting some new users; getting new users to participate in user-based evaluation of the interactive prototype of the food app

- having new users complete the priming activity with the question: how do I feel about food preparation and planning?

- running user-based testing with between 8 and 12 users once the interactive prototype is developed (number to be decided based on feedback received)

- splitting days of testing so that we can integrate feedback and refine designs as we go, before finalizing the design for testing and development cycles ahead of the launch; for example, one day of testing, three days to update designs; one day of testing, three days to update designs, and so on

Preparing Materials

There's no need to prepare all the materials for the user-focused activities across the project right now, but we do need to create the recruitment specification as a priority so we can get the contextual inquiries up and running. We can reuse this recruitment brief for all phases of research in our project and, as previously mentioned, you can find the one I created in the tools section of this book called **chapter03/recruitment-specification-template.dotx**. We'll also need to organize tools for the sessions at some point. For now, our priorities are:

Prompts for contextual inquiries	For this, we take our initial questions from the section called "Ten Questions to Kick Off this Project" in Chapter 2 and add our expanded questions covered earlier; then we edit it down to one page so that it's not intrusive.
Sign-off and agreement for use of data	Take a look at the example template, **chapter03/consent-form-template.dotx**, in the tools section of this book. This permits us to use the information we collect. It's also a good place to have the sign-off for receiving the cash incentive we provide to them.

Research considerations

When investigating how participants prepare, store, and share information relating to food and meal preparation, we need to remember:

- We're interested in contexts of use within people's homes: how they behave in the kitchen and work with recipe information, as well as how they prepare food and share via online channels.

- We should schedule two or three contextual inquiries per day maximum to allow for travel between locations.

- We are willing to pay $200 per person for participating in a contextual inquiry and completing a priming homework activity before seeing them. This is quite generous in terms of incentives, but keep in mind that they'll be preparing a meal that we'll then eat together at the end of the session. I always find that you get what you pay for when it comes to incentivizing participants—the more you offer, the more effort you see from users on tasks like homework.

- It's critical to gain permission from participants to use the information as we want .

What next?

We then recruited people based on our expectations of who our users would be, and how many we'd like to talk to. The next part in our cooking app journey was to visit the actual users.

Contextual Reflections

What are your thoughts on this chapter, and how will they shape what you might do next time? Based on the outcomes, how might you approach your next project differently?

The Scene Is Set

In this chapter, we have taken some time to understand the business problem we are faced with, and we've crafted a UX process for research that will help us design with a level of empathy for the eventual users of our product. Once you go to the user's environment and make an assessment of what matters most to them, you need to then move toward making sense of what you have seen.

Next up, we'll look at how to analyze all that data we've now collected and see how it may indeed change our design approach, and propel us further forward.

Recap of What You Need to Know

Going into the users world:

- Remember you are not your users; you will always uncover surprising revelations that will better inform your design process.

- Users are not designers, so don't expect them to solve your design problem—you'll still need to do that.

- Use methods that take you to their context in this early stage of exploration.

- A combination of methods works best, so try to pick more than one way to engage with your users across the course of your project.

Choosing the right UX methods:

- First clarify the questions you are focusing on; never conduct research without a clear idea of what you want to learn from it (use the 5 Whys).

- Choose the appropriate research mode to suit the questions you want to answer; different research methods can help you to uncover:

- what people think (survey focus groups)

- what someone is trying to accomplish (contextual inquiry, diary study, interviews)

- what tasks someone is trying to complete (user-based testing, design workshops)

- Consider selectively posting questions to a group of people via social media.

- Engaging with users will look something like this:

  - Know what you want to ask users.

  - Create an outline of who you want to talk to.

  - Plan the method you'll follow to engage users throughout your project.

  - Create a recruitment brief and recruit your users (either through your client, or your own methods).

  - Go see the users and gather insights from the experience.

Recruiting the right people:

- Try to create behaviorally focused criteria for your user recruitment process that homes in on user tasks, as well as demographic information. To do this:

  - brainstorm tasks

  - group these into clusters

  - assign a name to broad user segments

  - use demographic information to enhance your personas

- Go a little left of center in your recruitment to consider the edge cases associated with your product or service, and try to include these in your research.

- Priorities change and that's okay. The project will continue to be an important vehicle for you to evolving your thinking and clarify the right outcomes.

- Fail fast and fail early should be your mantra; good designers don't expect to get it right the first time.

Chapter

4

Making Sense of What You've Found

In previous chapters, we've focused on the research phase of our UX framework. This has concentrated on understanding the business problem (in Chapter 2) and user context (in Chapter 3), so that you may use this information to direct your project work.

It's important to consider human needs early on in your design life cycle, so that you can transform these ideas into new products or design features. Allowing proper time for analysis and synthesis of your research is the significant step between research and design, and this is what we'll cover in this chapter: the **insights phase**, illustrated in Figure 4.1.

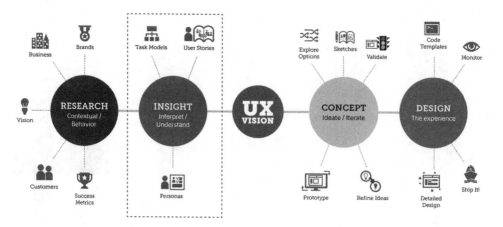

Figure 4.1. Insight phase: Making sense of your findings

We will focus on three critical elements: extracting information from data and transforming it, creating opportunities from insights, and benefiting from behavior design. We will discuss that gray area between going into a person's home and being exposed to their world, and then staring at your data and deciding how to connect the dots in a meaningful way. Your project (and designs) will be better for this experience.

What to Do with All That Data

We're not done with research yet; there's still some to conduct in the latter stages of our UX process (namely, the concept and design phases). This chapter, however, represents the first step in analyzing what we've collected.

 Watch Getting Ahead of Yourself

The process of formulating your own hypothesis based on the combination of sources is known as synthesis. It is the end-point of your analysis activities that allows you to turn new and interesting thoughts into tangible—and often innovative—ideas for products, services, or systems.

As a result of all this thinking, your data analysis actually begins well before you find yourself staring at a bunch of written notes or transcripts—and this is good!

You are right where you need to be, but still some way from having made total sense of it all, as illustrated by Figure 4.2.

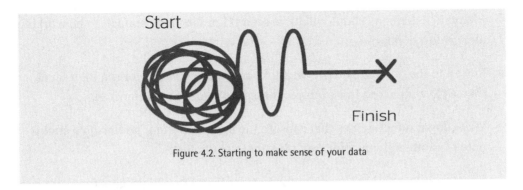

Figure 4.2. Starting to make sense of your data

Where to start?

There are a couple of post-research tasks that I recommend. First, there are the tasks you should perform immediately after a day of sessions that help you keep your data organized and communication channels open. Then there are the more reflective tasks to be performed at the conclusion of all sessions, which we'll discuss in a moment. A variety of documentation items are shown in Figure 4.3.

Figure 4.3. Documentation can take different forms

Immediately after each day of sessions, I do the following:

- Maintain a dialogue about what I've seen if I'm fortunate enough to be working alongside a colleague.

- Return to the office and write on sticky notes of a given color the high-level themes I've observed (for example, blue for themes I am inferring).

- Write down direct quotes that capture the most important stories on a sticky note of another given color (say pink for user quotes).

- Shoot a daily email to the client (or broader team) that highlights the day's key themes. These are always sent with the caveat that they are initial observations only, but it's a nice way to share the stories as you proceed with them, as it keeps the client involved in your process.

This early documentation keeps insights fresh and the details safe as you move through your hectic schedule of visiting users in their natural environment.

Get Your Stationery On

There seems to be a few standard tools of the insight phase that most UX professionals use. Shown in Figure 4.4, these are basic items of stationary such as sticky-notes, marker pens, butchers paper, highlighter pens, and index cards.

Figure 4.4. Meet your new friends

These materials are helpful when you're trying to make sense of the data you collect. They enable you to break down paragraphs of dialogue from observation into more discrete units (the first real step of your analysis process). Doing this allows you to shift around specific details that relate to particular examples, as well as remove irrelevant detail or general noise. Information transferred to sticky-notes is easier to manipulate and combine with insights from others on your team. Clustering and towering allows you to rethink the data, helping patterns to emerge and opportunities to be identified.

Creating a Common Project Space

Once you've completed all the user visits in your schedule, you should now (if you've yet to do so) create a space in your office for all your notes and user information.

This **common project space** will help facilitate discussions that are out of the way of others in the organization; it becomes a place to meet and brainstorm with people in your team. Even if you work on your own, you can't underestimate the value of putting information on the wall, making it visible, staring at it, and thinking about it.

Having visual prompts in your workspace helps to trigger ideas; you should also add to the wall your initial A3 summaries of your client's business, which you created in the section called "A Framework" in Chapter 2.

This first cut of information that goes up on the wall are the notes you made as you went, along with any photos of the participants or priming activities they have completed, as seen in Figure 4.5.

Figure 4.5. Start adding information to the wall

Reviewing Your Notes

Your next priority is to review your notes, read over transcripts, or revise any video footage shot. Regardless of the format you recorded information in, now is the time to transfer it to sticky-notes or any format that you can easily manipulate by moving it around and looking for patterns.

I prefer to take notes by writing direct quotations from the user's mouth, because it prevents me from making inferences from what I hear in the wild. There have been a few situations where I've written down something seemingly insightful at the time, only to reread it later and be unable to understand it.

The data remains true to what you've heard when you follow a note-taking practice of writing down direct quotes, and it also keeps you focused on user behavior.

Process of Affinity Mapping

Transferring information to a new format in order to move it around really helps to identify themes and tease out patterns, and makes it easier to collaborate with other team members or your client.

Once your notes are on the wall, your first priority is to make it more manageable, and this basically entails clustering like items. This is what is often referred to as **affinity mapping** or the affinity diagramming process.[1] Affinity mapping visually associates the data in some way, usually in towers or groupings. How you arrange the information is less important than the order and associations you impose on your data.

The benefits of affinity mapping is that it allows you to:

- group, review, and transform the findings as you continue analyzing the data

- refine the information and remove the noise

- home in on key themes, patterns of behavior, and emergent opportunities from the data

Figure 4.6 shows some of the benefits of affinity mapping.

Figure 4.6. Reviewing and refining the data collaboratively

---

[1] It is also referred to as the KJ Method, named after Jiro Kawakita who defined this practice in the 1960s.

Invite Others into Your Process

It's often useful to invite your client to review the findings at this early stage and discuss what you've seen, sharing anecdotes as you go. It brings the research process to life for them and helps them see how ideas are generated from the research.

Often, not enough time or focus is given to the analysis stage of a project due to the fact that it remains largely invisible to your client; involving them in this process helps them to see how the research outcomes will positively impact your design work.

Insights into Opportunities

An important part of reviewing the data is to relay to others what you've seen, what you think this means, and what the design implications might be. It may seem basic enough, but the more people you can discuss your data with, the better off your final result will be. Verbalizing the findings forces you to explain it, so you are in effect making sense of it for yourself too. It forces you to review your assumptions and challenge your approach and interpretation of the data.

This is where sketching through possibilities can also be a useful way to explore the insights you discover.

Using Sketching to Explore Possibilities

Sketch solutions when you are feeling inspired; it might not provide the answer, but act more as a vehicle towards deeper understanding. An example is shown in Figure 4.7.

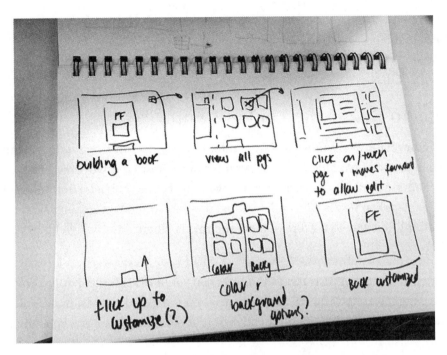

Figure 4.7. Sketching through some options

As tempting as it might be, don't assume you've nailed your first sketch and start creating a polished visual. It will be far more costly to find out later that your initial approach was the wrong way to go.

As you—individually or as a group—consider solutions and strategies, you'll find yourself circling back and forward and, more than likely, coming back to the same few ideas that have weight and power. It's amazing how worthwhile ideas continually bubble to the top. Make sure you listen to what this tells you about where you should head in your design efforts.

There Are No Bad Ideas Right Now

This is always said in reference to design, but there are no bad ideas at this point. Try to generate as many ideas as you can, because it's unclear what the right path might be, and this stage of the process is about exploration.

Discuss your reasoning, and encourage everyone to build on what's presented rather than shooting anything down. Use statements such as "what I like about that is ..." (to build on a positive), or "extending this idea ..." (to push a good idea forward), or "yes, and ..." (expanding on an idea that comes up). If you see the situation differently to others, watch the language you use, as it's necessary to embrace ideas and generate as many as possible right now, as opposed to shutting down conversation with "I disagree ...".

What to Be on the Lookout For

When going back over your notes from interviews or user-testing sessions, look out for when participants have created shortcuts or their own way of doing tasks. Consider their motivations and drivers; observe their habits and behavior, the spoken and the unspoken needs. This tells you where they might be seeking a better or more simplified way to perform a task, and this is where your design efforts can be usefully focused.

Recently, I conducted research in the financial services sector. A pattern emerged where people were putting all their expenses on their credit cards, in order to have all their transactions documented and sent to them monthly as one consolidated view.

This told me that the standard breakup of accounts was unhelpful, and that people preferred one view to better manage their finances. This system workaround by customers formed the basis of one of our design sessions, which looked to resolve this issue for banking customers.

Identifying Unexpected Opportunities

Opportunities are the changes we can envisage based on what we've heard or seen in our research efforts. These are the stories about the way people live or work, and the gaps we see between the present and the future state that will make their lives easier.

Quite often the nature of research is to uncover elements that weren't part of the original brief, yet might significantly benefit your client's business if you were to use it.

A project I worked on some years ago involved the merge of two Interactive Voice Response (IVR) systems. The original brief was to come up with a new blueprint for the system. As we conducted research into the existing systems and crafted the new solution, we realized that a really basic point had been overlooked by both systems: neither IVR system catered to noncustomers.

The IVR's menu only catered to existing customers, as a customer number was needed to access the menu. This made it impossible for potential customers to inquire about the company's products or services.

We took this research insight and ensured both new and existing customers were able to find the information they needed from the main menu. A great result was achieved, with customers being able to more easily access the system, and the business gaining a 40% increase in product purchases via the call center.

So how do you make sure you extrapolate when interpreting opportunities from the data? One way is to continually ask yourself:

> "Based on what we now know about the users and their environment, what does a [new way of living and behaving] look like?"

This shifts data analysis beyond direct observations and reported findings towards the design phase, with the hope of closing whatever design gaps might exist.

 What is a design gap?

The design gap happens as a result of flaws in the design process, leaving a range of basic human needs unmet. Clients might be unable to express their needs; the vision might be unclear; the designers might not listen to what's said, or bias what they hear to conform to their own assumptions. There's an interesting article by Elliot Felix on the design gap in the context of architecture in *The Journal of Design Strategies*, Vol. 4, No. 1, Spring 2010.[2]

A significant benefit of the UX process is that it narrows the likelihood of user needs being inadequately met or client needs being misinterpreted in a design project.

Moving into Ideation

Ideation (in this context, short for idea generation) involves taking the opportunities and insights from research and turning them into a question that the design process explores and resolves.

---

[2] http://www.degw.com/press_article.aspx?id=60&name=Closing+the+Design+Gap&a=1

The more you structure insights from your research, the more guidance is provided to the design team (and clarity to you). You're able to show your client the most valuable research insights that should be explored in your design conception stage. It's the perfect opportunity to demonstrate the link between research and design.

Simply pose the question "how do we ..." or "how can we ..." before the statements of opportunity. This invites further discussion with your team and client about which areas you want to explore further (and which ones you don't).

As an example, we might deduce the following from research:

Observation   People flip between the ingredients list and the directions when cooking. This means that the cooking process is stop-start, with cooks often losing their place on the page and being frustrated with having to find it again.

Opportunity   Allow people to seamlessly move between ingredients and directions when cooking.

Ideation   How can we allow people to move seamlessly between reviewing ingredients and directions when cooking?

It's important at this stage to encourage your client and others to set aside any business constraints and think strategically about "what could be." Later on as you refine your thinking and try to prioritize ideas is when you should consider constraints.

A handy way to prioritize is to think of reasons why you should support further exploration of an opportunity, as well as arguments against it.

Furthermore, it can be useful to consider how different areas of the business might be impacted by your findings and insights, so either pull some of them along for the ride, or drag out your original A3 sheet and refer to this in your brainstorming efforts.

Analysis Paralysis

There are going to be times in the analysis process when you'll feel quite overwhelmed and drowning in data. This is affectionately referred to as analysis paralysis.

There's a lot of information to face in the insights phase. It is messy and hard, and often you can be still unsure if what you think is right. Even knowing when to stop and call it a day can be tricky to work out, as Figure 4.8 illustrates.

Figure 4.8. Analysis paralysis can occur to the best of us

When you're feeling this way, bring a new person into the fold and pitch it to them.

Pitching what you understand up to this point forces you to reiterate what you think the main insights are, and why you believe they are even insights at all. This often helps you to rethink your viewpoint and rebuild your arguments, if necessary.

Your ideas will continue to evolve for the duration of the project, and because UX is human-centered and prototype-driven, you'll be able to revisit your assumptions and test these with your users to make sure your hunches are on the right track. You just need to have enough understanding and bright ideas to help shape the way forward.

Communicating Your Outcomes to Others

Don't be afraid to share your insights across the business and gauge the reaction. Organizations everywhere are grappling with how to deliver a great experience across many different channels; what you've come across during research is bound to identify several points of contact with your client's company and ways in which the organization can improve services in the eyes of the customer.

Invest some time in visualizing your outcomes or creating short-cut clips of video footage so that the user's voice is clearly conveyed. It helps bring to life the problems and stories you've observed, and is the best way I've seen to get everyone on the same page. This will help to communicate the results of your research to a wider audience.

Understanding Behavior Design

In earlier chapters, we've discussed the importance of technology as an agent for shifting or influencing human behavior. The challenge as designers and developers, however, is to understand what actually makes people behave a certain way in the first place.

How do we start to unpack our data to focus on habits and behavior?

Fogg Behavior Model

B.J. Fogg was the first to properly discuss the power of technology in persuading humans to do tasks they might not have ordinarily bothered to do.[3]

The expansion of the smartphone market hails a revolutionary time for behavior change through design of technology. This is largely due to the unprecedented access to information we enjoy over super-fast networks.

There are many models of behavior change, but I think Fogg's is the simplest to understand. It also explains behavior change within the technology context, so let's review it to help you consider behavior-based insights from your data.

In the Fogg Behavior Model,[4] behavior consists of three elements: motivation, ability, and a trigger. Figure 4.9 explains that to observe behavior change, all three elements must be present. Remember the formula: B=MAT, where B is behavior, M is motivation, A is ability, and T is a trigger.

---

[3] I recommend you have a look at B.J. Fogg's landmark book, *Persuasive Technology: Using Computers to Change What We Think and Do* (San Francisco: Morgan Kaufmann, 2003), particularly Chapter 8.
[4] http://www.behaviormodel.org/

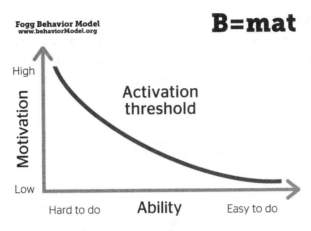

Figure 4.9. The Fogg Behavior Model

In Chapter 2, we thought about the behavior we wanted to change in our users, and looked at the A-B-C model of behavior change. Now look at your collected data and think about the users' current behavior:

- Do they have the motivation to do what you're asking of them?
- Do they have the ability to do what you are asking of them?
- How would you trigger the behavior you want to see? When would you trigger it?

Let's dissect the model a little more to understand the different elements within it.

Motivation

Motivation corresponds to basic human needs and often relates to an end-state ideal or a goal that a person feels compelled to achieve (think of losing weight or getting fit as examples).

As Fogg sees it, core motivators tend to fit into one of the following categories:

- sensation (pleasure and pain)
- expectation (hope and fear)
- belonging (acceptance and rejection)

Ultimately, motivation is the degree to which the person wants the behavior to happen. Traditionally, it can be a hard one to influence, but technology is changing that.

Consider this example from LinkedIn in Figure 4.10. Having an incomplete profile causes friction in our quest to create order. Logging on and seeing that your profile is incomplete is disruptive, and LinkedIn has capitalized on this very well, nudging you to do what they want you to do: complete the profile.

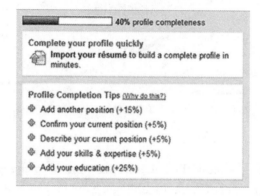

Figure 4.10. The disruption of an incomplete profile

So what comes next when your profile is 100% complete? No doubt there will be other prompts or calls-to-action to keep you doing what they want you to do.

Ability

Ability essentially represents how hard or easy it is to perform a certain action. What this dimension really refers to is simplicity and this is essentially what UX is about.

A classic example of restricting users' ability is the practice of forcing users to register or log on in order to proceed with their task. This is particularly frustrating when there is no opt-out, and time and again I have watched users abandon important tasks in testing sessions, such as purchasing an item when shopping online.

Every time a user abandons a task on an ecommerce site, a sale is lost. That's why Amazon made it dead-simple and introduced the "1-Click" shopping service, as seen in Figure 4.11.

Figure 4.11. Make it easy for me to spend my money

I am a total sucker for very clever design like this.

A software product that makes it easy to perform a task will be more successful in convincing its users to perform that task. Fogg notes that simplicity is the key ingredient that ultimately changes behaviors.

In terms of your research data, consider where the blocker to the ideal behavior you are designing for exists, and aim to make that process easy to complete in your design efforts, in order to observe behavior change.

Triggers

Motivation and ability are only two parts of the story; you also need a trigger that prompts the person to action.

Triggers activate behavior; for example:

- the phone rings → you answer it
- your alarm goes off in the morning → you turn it off (and get up, with a little luck)
- email arrives in your inbox → you read it

Triggers can be sneaky too. For example, when I first sit at my desk in the morning, I have an instant urge for a coffee. If I see a macaroon, I need one. In the technology space, push notifications on my cell make me check my phone—sometimes in a manner that could be likened to addiction.

The list of triggers that prompt you to behave in a certain way goes on and on. Take Figure 4.12, for instance.

Figure 4.12. Snack time anyone?

Putting Hot Triggers in the Path of Motivated People

The Fogg Behavior Model highlights that a trigger is what makes behavior happen (in conjunction with motivation and ability). What does this mean for data analysis and opportunities for your design work?

There is an opportune moment to prompt the behavior you want to observe in someone. A trigger occurring at that moment will cause behavior changes in your users. Once this trigger is in place, you can begin to create habits.

 ### The Opportune Moment

Kairos is an ancient Greek word meaning the right or opportune moment; the moment of indeterminate time of a special occurrence.

In persuasive design, the opportune moment is the instant a person is prompted into action by an element in your design. It is also the time when they are most likely to comply with your intent.

When designing, ask yourself: when is the *kairos* for your user? When are they most motivated and most likely to act in the way you intend? You need to understand the impulse and design around it.

Making Behavior Change Happen

According to the Fogg Behavior Model, there is a threshold where behavior change will or won't happen. For change to occur, we need to focus our efforts wisely on those users who are motivated to change; otherwise behavior change becomes difficult to realize.

Ultimately, our users:

- need to notice the trigger
- should associate the trigger with the target behavior (for example, my morning coffee at my desk)
- are motivated when the trigger occurs and are able to act

People are using and responding to technology-based triggers every day when they interact with social media platforms such as Facebook and Twitter. It's fair to say that social media is the best example of persuasive design available, and with the proliferation of it on smartphones, this has really upped the ante.

Persuasive Design: The Ideal Hot Trigger

Social media taps ingeniously into the social motivators of recognition, belonging, comparison, peer pressure, reciprocity, cooperation, competition, control—the list goes on.[5]

If there's an email in my inbox via Facebook that says I've been tagged in a photo, or a Twitter notification that a person has commented on what I've tweeted, I tend to click through to check it out. The Twitter page shown in Figure 4.13 demonstrates these motivators (highlighted with ticks) in action.

For example, we like to see what others are saying, and we respond (reciprocity); we're shown how many friends and followers we have (recognition, visibility); we feel pressure from the comments and opinions of others, and are compelled to comment (call to action, peer pressure, competition).

The list of persuasive factors within this page alone is staggering.

---

[5] B.J. Fogg, *Mass Interpersonal Persuasion: An Early View of a New Phenomenon*, (San Francisco: Stanford University, 2008)

Figure 4.13. Social media, the hottest trigger of them all

So how does this all fit together?

If a person has motivation and enough ability, and a trigger is presented at the right time, it's highly likely they'll perform that task you want them to do. Check out B.J. Fogg's website for more on triggers.[6]

In the Fogg Behavior Model, there's a **behavior threshold**. If you provide a trigger to the person above the threshold, you'll be successful. Send them a trigger below that threshold, and your trigger will fail, as indicated in Figure 4.14.

---

[6] http://www.behaviormodel.org/triggers.html

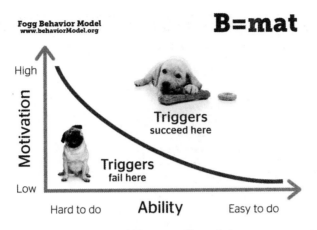

Figure 4.14. Focus your efforts wisely

Remember the formula B=MAT. For the desired behavior to occur, all three factors have to be present at the same time.

So what if we want to create a new behavior? What is the most important factor to focus our efforts on? Do we focus on triggers, motivation, or ability?

Where should we focus our efforts?

The answer is ability. Ability is much easier to manipulate than motivation. Changing people's minds is tricky, so motivation is the hardest to effect. The irony is that a marketing budget is usually focused on swaying attitudes, even when we know that people often don't know why they do things and have a hard time verbalizing what they do.

As we saw in the section called "Fogg Behavior Model", it is possible to drive action—even if your user's motivation is low—just by making it easy. This is a vital point, and goes some way towards explaining why simplicity matters more than anything else in your design work.

The example from Yammer in Figure 4.15 reinforces this. I've had an incomplete profile on Yammer for a long time and ignored it. Why? Because it takes effort for me to update, and I can't be bothered—it's not that important to me.

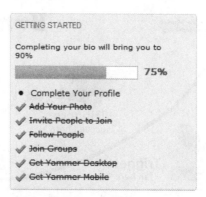

Figure 4.15. Make updating your profile stupidly simple

Take that effort away, however, and we start to see profiles that are 100% complete. This was the case with the LinkedIn example previously mentioned, which only required me to respond with a yes or no.

Noticing Behaviors and Habits

As I mentioned at the start of the chapter, focus on expected (or unexpected) workarounds or shortcuts that illustrate how people handle imperfect situations or environments. This will reveal how your design work might help solve these problems for them (narrowing the design gap).

You need to look carefully for this information. Often people are unaware that the workarounds they've formulated are awkward; they employ them automatically and often without complaint—just as they accept the technology or environment and work around it.

This reinforces why behavioral observation in your work is critical.

Simplicity: the Secret Sauce in Behavior Design

Removing complexity is necessary when persuading people to change their behavior. Make performing tasks stupidly simple and people will generally do what it is that you want them to do.

Case Study: Collecting the Ingredients

Conducting contextual research in our users' homes allowed us to see what cooking meant to potential users of the app. It also gave us insight into how they managed and stored recipe information, how and what they cooked, and what their habits and behaviors associated to cooking were generally.

As part of the contextual research, I had our participants cook for me, which enabled me to see them in cooking action. I was able to quietly observe their processes, and see whether they relied (or not) on a recipe from a book, as witnessed in Figure 4.16.

Figure 4.16. Watching users in context

Overall, this approach worked well, but on reflection more time should have been spent at each house. Three hours per house wasn't enough, and two in one day was too much. Given our tight time frames, I was fitting in the research as quickly as I could over weeknights and one weekend so that we didn't delay our design process.

It was an enjoyable experience that revealed a number of insights in a relatively quick time frame. They were also great cooks!

Having four participants, we scheduled the research at odd times of the day: Saturday breakfast, Sunday lunch, Friday late afternoon for dinner, and Thursday evening dinner. The purpose was to gain a feel for how different days of the week impacted meal preparation and selection. This allowed me to gauge how the user felt about the meal preparation time, how it impacted on what they made, and their reasons for it.

We would not have gained these insights had we just met users during the week or only in the daytime. Looking outside standard time frames for further insights is worth considering in your research projects.

As with any project, you need to keep on top of the evaluation process, jotting down the key points as seen in Figure 4.17. During the case study, I'd produce themes from these and then relay to the app team the stories as I was hearing them. We'd then talk about what it all meant in the context of the design and the features that might make a difference for people using the app.

Figure 4.17. Keeping on top of analysis

As a team, we immersed ourselves in the world of food and recipes, scattering various cooking artifacts around the office.

Others in our office not involved in our research were bringing in their favorite cookbooks for inspiration, family recipe scrapbooks they had kept for years, and cookbooks that family members had given them as gifts. We even hijacked my mother's recipe folder and index card box of recipes—seen in Figure 4.18—so that we could have quick access to them for reference.

Figure 4.18. Recipe stores provide constant inspiration

Whenever we faced a design decision, we found ourselves looking to all our recipe information and storage systems in addition to the research outcomes.

This brings us to crunch time for the data analysis and synthesis process.

Collating the Data after Research

After the data-gathering process, we followed the standard format of affinity mapping to make sense of what we saw, and to create order from the information and insights. The first task was to review some of the common themes, patterns, or ideas that emerged at this stage of the process.

These insights are the first step in analyzing and synthesizing the large volume of data collected, and forms the start of the overall synthesis process. They are intentionally high-level at this point as they're intended to give a quick view across the users seen, and then be used as input to the ideation process (which we'll cover shortly).

What themes or patterns were observed?

Here's a sample of the insights we recorded:

- Users had a variety of ways to manage their recipe information, and none of them were particularly satisfactory to the users.

- Many users relied on websites, friends, family, or cookbooks and magazines for meal inspiration, as depicted in the priming activity in Figure 4.19.

- Only recipes accompanied by an image stood a chance of being selected.

- Meal planning occurred on the weekend for the majority of people, as it enabled them to shop and plan for the week ahead.

- Meal planning enabled busy singles and families to be organized, shop efficiently, and reduce food wastage—ultimately saving money.

Figure 4.19. Participants' priming activity

- Cooking patterns differed on weekdays compared to weekends. People who loved to cook all day on the weekend focused on quick and simple meals during the week, as they were time poor and cooking became a necessity, as opposed to a passion.

- The sharing of recipes occurred via a number of ways: taking a photograph on a smartphone, emailing a recipe, printing out or photocopying a friend's recipe, sharing recipes via Facebook messaging, and family or friends writing out recipes on paper or in books.

- Printed or handwritten recipes were often lost, so users would ask their friends/family to resend them, or rewrite it. Recipes printed from a web source would be searched for and printed out again. Many users anticipated losing recipes, so would bookmark web pages to cover themselves.

- Most users only glanced at the recipe they were cooking, and only one user had yet to cook the recipe.

- All users had a collection of cookbooks and magazines, as well as a personal recipe scrapbook (such as that in Figure 4.20) filled with special recipes that had been tried and proven over time.

Figure 4.20. A scrapbook that houses special recipes

- Only firm favorites that had been cooked several times were included in the scrapbook. The majority of these were handwritten, though some were cut-outs that had been stuck to the pages.

- Many of the written-down recipes were titled according to their source; for example, "Auntie Judy's Scones" or "Dad's Bolognaise."

- Showing love through the food prepared and served was a common theme.

- It was quite common for foodie friends to evaluate dishes they'd cooked and share opinions amongst each other.

- There was a tendency for users to have secret recipes.

- Some users were happy to share, while others had to consider whether the person interested in their recipe deserved it.

- Cooking was a form of escapism, letting people focus on countries they'd been to or wanted to visit, all without leaving their living room.

- Recipes took users back to a time and place in their past, and cooking the dish kept the memory alive for them.

What were our insights and design ideas?

As outlined earlier in this chapter, the ideation process is about producing opportunities out of observations, and then brainstorming how you can facilitate a certain action with the design idea, as shown in Figure 4.21.

Figure 4.21. Ideating on what we saw

Research analysis should take place immediately after the research is done, but analysis of what you've seen will continue throughout the project as you design concepts, workshop ideas with your client or team, and engage users again down the track.

Some of the themes we observed after research led to insights that we turned into design concepts for the app. These helped us to ascertain the overall design framework, and also identify the app's "killer features," which are outlined here:

Secrecy of recipes

Insight:

There's a lot of heritage tied up in recipes.

Sharing recipes with people other than family or close friends is inconceivable for some users.

What we know:

We can make the book invitation only.

It is technically possible to offer locked areas.

Design Idea:

Sharing my book: App must allow user to select who they give access to.

Keep to myself: App must enable user to lock recipes as they create them.

Exclusivity associated with access to recipes

Insight:

Being given access to secret recipes is held in high esteem.

It is also special to be given a favorite recipe.

There is status associated with others knowing you were given a secret recipe.

What we know:

We can show who has access to recipes (both secret and general) among a list of friends.

We can allow exclusive access to locked recipes.

Notifications can allow others to keep track of activity.

Design Idea:

Gifting a recipe: Make a big deal over a secret or locked recipe being shared. It can involve gifting a secret or standard recipe.

App must allow users to gift recipes to others, and allow visibility of this process to all friends linked to a user's book via notification.

A physical book

Insight:

Most users have a special recipe book to which they regularly add.

This book is different to files of loose recipes used only for inspiration and printed books or magazines.

What we know:

We can recreate the book metaphor in the app, allowing page flips and sharing of others' "books."

Design Idea:

> *Replicating a physical book*: The app must appear like a book and behave like a book.

> Allow the books to be ordered, printed, and sent to the owner or gifted to family/friends to give a physical offline reason to start creating recipes in the app.

> The overall experience of unboxing the printed book and how it is presented is critical to continuing the experience.

Recipes from the Web

Insight:

> Many users locate and search for recipes via the Web.

> These are often referred to in cooking, but lost if printed out.

What we know:

> There are sites that will allow us to copy their content across and then reformat to our recipe template in one press of a button.

Design Idea:

> *Search and copy recipes from the Web*: App must allow users to search for recipes online, copy recipes to the book, and reformat in the book's standard layout and design.

Reading recipe on a mobile device

Insight:

> Several users cook from recipes they find on the Web via their mobile devices (tablets or smartphones) instead of cookbooks.

> Users are frustrated by having to repeatedly unlock the screen when it auto-locks.

> The majority of users are unaware they can change the auto-lock function to **Never** in their smartphone's general settings.

What we know:

It's possible to program a screen to override the time-out function in the native device when open.

Design Idea:

Screen lock for recipe card page: When the user hits the recipe card page, it must override standard settings and prevent the page from dimming or auto-locking.

Photo-upload a recipe

Insight:

Taking photos of handwritten recipes (especially family recipes) preserves family history and memories.

What we know:

It's desirable to upload photo images of recipes to then be used as the main recipe text.

Design Idea:

Photo upload: The app must enable uploading a photo image of food, as well as reformatting the image as the main recipe detail.

There are many more insights that came from our research efforts not documented here for practicality reasons; still, I hope you can see the value of conducting contextual research and the design ideas that we may have otherwise overlooked.

Knowledge Is Power

In this chapter, we've covered that gray area of making sense of what you saw when you were out in the field conducting research.

We reviewed several tactical approaches to synthesizing your data, and also examined the Fogg Behavior Model on behavior change as a way to further clarify why people behave and act in a certain way. Finally, we discussed how to use this information to assist in your design efforts.

In Chapter 5, we'll be moving into the concept design phase, where we'll examine sketching as a tool and explore different design options. Then we'll begin prototyping and refining our ideas, where we'll validate them once again with users.

Recap of What You Need to Know

What to do with all that data:

- You've probably already been making sense of your data before the insights phase, and this will continue throughout the UX process.

- Tools of the insight phase include:
  - wall space for putting up your data
  - markers, highlighters, and other pens
  - butchers paper (if you want to move it around)
  - sticky-notes

- Immediately after research you should:
  - transfer your notes to sticky-notes
  - pull out quotes and stories
  - identify themes and send a summary to your client
  - put all these up on the wall to manipulate and transform (using affinity mapping)

- In your data look for:
  - shortcuts
  - habits
  - tasks that are repeated
  - unexpected or unusual features
  - noise (to remove)

Shifting from insights to opportunities:

- Go beyond mere observations or restating of facts by:
  - brainstorming with others and thinking out loud about what you see as the main patterns and themes
  - detecting patterns that occur more than once across data

- Identify opportunities and move to ideation by:
  - singling out the observations that are important
  - turning observations into statements of opportunity
  - ideating opportunities by adding "how can we ... "

- Use sketching to create meaning, reflect, and brainstorm.

- Watch out for analysis paralysis and brainstorm with people not involved in your research to help you back on track.

- Communicate your outcomes to others so that different areas of the business can deliver an improved experience to users.

Understanding behavior design:

- Designing for behavior change (or designing with intent) is what successful designers need to understand and incorporate into their work today. Successful technology understands users' habits or becomes a new trigger.

- Remember B.J. Fogg's B=MAT formula, where for behavior to occur there needs to be motivation, ability, and a trigger.

- Simplicity is the secret sauce in behavior design. If you make it simple, it will encourage even those low-motivation users to actually change their behavior.

5

Sketching to Explore the Design Concept

In Chapter 4, we discussed how to deal with moving data from observational research towards design insights to identify opportunities for your designs. Part of that discussion touched on sketching to help you understand the design problem, and in this chapter we'll look at sketching to help you explore a range of possible concepts.

Making designs that are easy, intuitive, and elegant takes a lot of thought, iteration, and refinement. The sketching process will help communicate your thoughts to others and solve problems visually, before you settle on a design approach to prototype and test (we'll cover prototyping and testing in Chapter 6).

At this stage, you're bound to have a few hunches regarding what will work. Sketching is testing, not refining; so your next step is to put your ideas on paper, so you can work through your alternatives and establish where to go from here. Finally, remember to test your ideas again with potential users.

How the Concept Phase Works

In the insight phase, we analyzed data collected from our user interactions in order to establish a clear design direction. However, there's still a bit of mess to sort through: there are many ways to interpret data and design a solution, so there are going to be questions and unknowns.

We'll continue to engage with users as a way to validate new ideas and gather feedback. As the design evolves and we arrive at a solution, we'll then prototype it to test out our thinking, as shown in Figure 5.1.

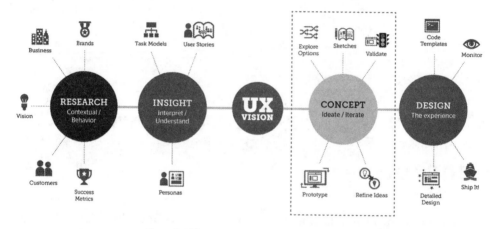

Figure 5.1. The concept phase: Starting to design

If you are anything like me, you'll probably be rolling over in your mind what you have seen. You'll no doubt question yourself and others—and this is important—as it will propel you towards a better outcome. The following quote, known as the Combinations Rule, sums it up for me:

> "Designing is basically the practice of combining stuff; ideally in ways that haven't been seen before. So the more stuff you know (about everything), the greater the chance you'll find a relevant and distinctive, and therefore effective (and original) combination."
>
> —Ace Jet 170[1]

---

[1] http://acejet170.typepad.com/foundthings/2007/03/uncommon_knowle_2.html

Sketching to Help You Think

Words can be open to misinterpretation when communicating your design ideas to others, as your client or co-workers might fill in the gaps with assumptions when they struggle to understand.

Designers are visual people, so you might have already started sketching after your first few meetings with the client. And as I suggested in Chapter 4, you might have even used sketching as a tool to help you understand and explore a deeper level of meaning in your research data.

This initial exploration can be done on your own to clarify your thinking, or with others to generate more ideas (we'll come to group sketching later in this chapter).

What are the benefits for my final design?

Sketching out your thoughts helps others see your thinking process and demonstrates what you're trying to say visually. Putting pen to paper often allows you to see the holes where the design might fail to work in practice, leading you to consider alternate solutions.

Drawing the solution also forces you to think about any constraints, and it is through these that you might reconsider features or functions for your product, and what they mean for your overall design.

At a high level, some of the benefits of sketching ideas at this stage of your project are that:

- you're able to quickly determine if your ideas will work quickly and inexpensively

- you can focus on one aspect at a time

- you'll be able to relinquish ideas that aren't working, as you've invested little time in them

- it helps you to consider several options, as many solutions might work at this stage

■ it brings your client along for the journey of the design process before any visual design hits the table.

The Evolution of Sketches

According to Bill Buxton, as your thinking evolves, the details of your sketches should advance, demonstrating a greater level of thinking.[2]

As a result, it becomes a "survival of the fittest" with your design ideas, as shown in Figure 5.2.

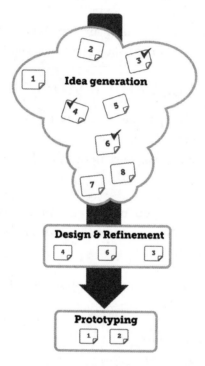

Figure 5.2. The design process is basically a survival of the fittest

Sketching is all about testing ideas, not refining. You should be thinking of the sketching process as an ideas generation stage, exploring a huge range of options and disposing of ideas that don't quite fit your design problem. The crux of sketching is about suggesting, exploring, questioning, and proposing; it is largely noncommittal.

---

[2] Bill Buxton's fabulous book, *Sketching User Experiences: Getting the Design Right and the Right Design* (San Francisco: Morgan Kaufmann, 2007), is well worth a read.

Bear in mind that sketches are not prototypes.

By the time you've refined your sketches to a few solid designs, you can approach the prototype stage. This is about testing the solutions that you're most confident with in order to finalize the design process ready for the build.

Prototyping a design takes more effort and overhead; the more confident you are with the design concept, the better. Think of sketching as the vehicle to propel you towards the right solution, as you explore the possibilities along the way.

There's No Need to Be an Artist

For those web geeks new to using the old-fashioned pen and paper, you might be thinking: "But I can't draw!"

You are not alone. In fact, many of the best designers I've worked with are quite rudimentary when it comes to sketching; it's more about communicating effectively to others rather than making it pretty.

Unfortunately, many people give up on sketching before they've even started, as they feel intimidated by the task. But don't be afraid of it, as it's intended to be basic, rough, and a long way from perfect.

The best way to overcome your fear is to start small with a straight line or two, and gain confidence through practicing. Doodle as you wait for the bus or watch TV.

Once you've progressed past straight lines, practice on simple objects that come up in your design work, such as people, emotions, or shapes. These are useful in UX work as they allow you to convey a bit of personality and meaning.

Avoid Losing Yourself in the Detail

It may work against you if you include too many inappropriate visual details. The bare bones of an idea that uses arrows, clouds, and straight lines to convey a rough user interaction is all you need to start you off, as seen in Figure 5.3.

As you become more confident with your drawing, you can add details along the way; this helps to give context to the design, but is not essential. What's most important is to just start sketching!

Figure 5.3. You don't need lots of detail initially

Exploring Interactions

As with other phases of the UX process, you might have started looking at competing products the minute you began the project. I usually do, and generally revisit this activity several times during the course of a design project, and especially when I start sketching.

Informed Innovation

You'll want to stay away from copycat design solutions; however, there is logic to understanding the way users interact and engage with similar products to help inform your early design process.

Look towards any heavily established conventions and seek to be original. But avoid swaying too far from standard conventions, as you might end up with a product that users will fail to understand.

Have a look around at what is out there and consider:

- What already exists that is similar?
- How is a parallel industry facing the problem you're looking at?
- What are the common patterns or metaphors that we wish to reflect?
- How can we learn from these examples to create a great experience for our users?

Learn from Good Examples

Scanning the landscape of competing products informs you of what is out there and can help reset your understanding of your users' expectations.

Reviewing how others have tackled similar design problems, or created successful examples of persuasive (even addictive) technology can help you with your own design solution. Familiarize yourself with a range of good and bad examples, and learn from what others have done as a way to guide some of your thinking.[3]

They often say there are no new ideas in the design world, and I think that is close to the truth. Styles come and go, or are reinvented through a new lens and successfully applied to new contexts. I think Mark Twain said it best: "History doesn't repeat itself—at best it sometimes rhymes."

Add to Your Wall of Information

As with the insight phase, creating a wall space for your inspiration activities examples helps to drive reflection and creativity. If you're working in a team, these spaces encourage hallway discussion as they help keep the focus of your design work top-of-mind, rather than filed away on your computer.

Based on what you find, you are often better able to isolate the design problem and discuss the scope of your product. The more you immerse yourself in the design problem and collaborate, the quicker you'll be on the same page as you progress.

If you work on your own, print out what you find and regularly contemplate these examples—such as in Figure 5.4—to evolve your thinking.

---

[3] B.J. Fogg's article, "Creating Persuasive Technologies: An Eight-step Design Process" (2009), highlights the need to learn from similar examples to help you create great design solutions. From Proceedings of PERSUASIVE 2009: Fourth International Conference on Persuasive Technology, Claremont, California, April 27-29, 2009, ACM Digital Library, New York

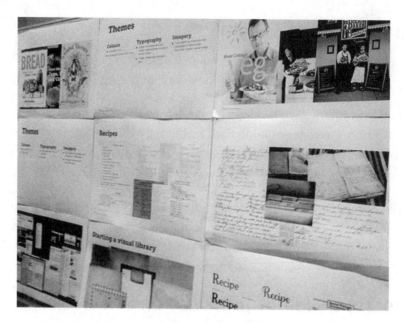

Figure 5.4. A shared place for design inspiration

Injecting the User's Voice

At some point in your project kick-off, your client has probably given you a range of documents that relate to the business and technical problems to be solved (for example, functional specifications, business goals, and other loose or fuzzy requirements discussed in meetings).

While they're a good reference point, in my experience they lack the user's voice. Instead, they focus heavily on back-end systems and business rules being fulfilled. While these documents should be considered, always remember that you are designing a solution for a *person*.

This is why scenarios are useful when you sketch. **Scenarios** are contextual descriptions of how a user interacts with an aspect of a product or service.

They allow you to consider the user's world in more detail, and visualize what it might be like to use a working model of your design, as Figure 5.5 demonstrates.

Figure 5.5. Remembering your user's world

Scenarios as a Design Tool

You need to understand the essence of your user's story in order to build up your designs. The benefit of scenarios is that they can be written in no time at all, and they're an effective way to communicate the design problem that needs to be solved.

 Walk Me Through It Again

In many ways, scenarios help us to understand different ways the future might unfold for users of the product or system. By sketching and (later) prototyping around scenarios, we validate our assumptions about how the final product should look, behave, and interact, giving the design a user focus.

Often, scenarios are just simple stories with several tasks that need to be completed by the end-user of the product or system.

Types of Scenarios

Use your research to help inform the scenarios you devise. Some types of scenarios include:

Context scenarios: explore how the product can best serve the needs of the user

Key pathway scenarios:	discuss the user's interactions with the product, focusing on how the user engages with it to achieve goals
Validation scenarios:	look at "what if" situations (edge cases) that might actually break the design (for example, chefs versus amateurs, restaurants versus market stalls)
Magic scenarios:	What if it was magic? Alan Cooper suggests imagining how a product can meet the needs of the user by pretending the interface is magic.[4] I love this idea, as it helps to generate discussion around what is possible without technology constraints.

 Recipe Role-play

What scenarios can you think of that might help shape the interactions that will be required of the recipe app?

Sketching from Your Personas' Point of View

Personas help you to shift your perspective and put yourself in another person's shoes. They can aid in bringing the user into conversations about products and services being designed. When sketching, personas are useful for considering interactions that matter most to a given user segment, (what would they want to see or do?).

Remember how we categorized users into personas for the purpose of recruitment in Chapter 3? At that time, our personas were fictitious and based on assumption; by now, we've interacted with people who we feel embody these original personas, and are able to offer more detail based on our field research. It's likely we'll merge several people we saw during that process when updating our personas, to bring them to life.

---

[4] *About Face: the Essentials of Interaction Design* by Alan Cooper, Robert Reimann, and David Cronin (Hoboken: Wiley, 2007).

When developing your personas, focus on behavior rather than demographics. What motivates and drives these user types, and what key activities do they typically perform (or not perform)? Give them a name, a personality, and a voice.

Here are some general points to keep in mind when finalizing your persona:

- Base them on contextual user research.

- Bring them to life by fleshing them out, including a name and photo.

- Include a defining quote from your research that personifies that user (remember all those quotes you wrote down during the research phase?).

- Document behaviors and drivers (tasks, wants, needs, goals, emotions).

- Have some basic demographics that link them to a specific internal market segment (shouldn't be the focus).

Combine Personas and Scenarios

Switching perspectives helps with lowering bias and leads to better decisions, just by considering a point of view other than our own.

Using personas in combination with different scenarios that you've created can support your initial design ideas and incorporate information about different user types.

When sketching and generating design ideas, refer to your personas and consider:

- What would [insert persona] think of this idea?
- How would [insert persona] react to this?
- Would [insert persona] use it?
- What would be useful to [insert persona]?

Exploring a range of scenarios through the eyes of different personas helps to refine design features you might explore in your concept work, and help with decisions for what you might leave out.

Ways to Approach Your Sketching

As you consider your interaction design problem, it is often helpful to move from high-level outlines of a user story to more detailed interactions.

Creating sketches provides a visual means to explain the logic behind your approach. Let's take a closer look at these different approaches now.

Storyboards

Storyboarding helps to focus a broader experience with a sequence of sketches that show how a design solution could work for your target audience. It shows how the user moves from one content area to another (or any kind of animation), much like a draft comic book or graphic novel.

This helps you to troubleshoot certain approaches, as shown in Figure 5.6, without investing too much time or effort fully designing or prototyping these interactions.

Figure 5.6. Storyboards communicate a wider context

Here are some tips to help you succeed:

- Ensure you have scenarios that are driving the storyboards, as they inform the storyboard's narrative. If the context for your storyboard is unclear or misunderstood by your team, you risk this exercise falling flat.

- Walk your team—or your client—through your thinking early and often; have them talk through your storyboard and annotate changes on your examples (red or green pens are great for "go" and "no go" annotations, as are sticky-notes).

- Make sure you capture your sketches on a canvas that can be placed on walls and moved around. Larger sticky-notes or index cards work well, as do A4 or A3 pages stuck on butchers paper.

- Stop refining when you feel that the big-picture framework is sound; then you can move down to the page-level interactions.

Ideas Generation

The whole point of sketching is to generate several possible approaches to solving your design problem, as illustrated in Figure 5.7. For example, how would the home screen of your product look like on a computer screen, compared to a tablet device or smartphone? This is helpful for considering which elements are truly essential to the overall experience, and what can be removed from your design.

You need to be brave enough to remove aspects of your design work that you might think are essential and immovable. This exercise can challenge you to do just this—remove, and then remove again—but take care to ensure nothing breaks.

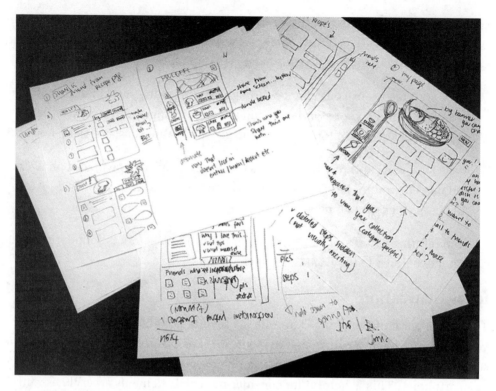

Figure 5.7. Rapidly generating lots of ideas

Here are some further tips when you reach this stage:

- Concentrate on a specific screen or feature of your product, and design it from as many angles as you can.

- Give yourself short bursts of time (for example, ten minutes) to come up with as many options as possible. This helps to create a sense of urgency about producing multiple options rather than perfecting just one.

- Post the options up on the wall, consider which features work and which don't, and encourage feedback from others on your team; this is a useful way to rapidly eliminate the ideas with no legs to stand on.

Sequencing

The pain you feel with an unusable product is usually the reflection of a poorly thought-out sequence of screens that merge together to make what is often referred to as the workflow or task flow of a product or service.

Start sketching the task flow sequence as early as possible to explore the logic of stepping a user through the process you've crafted. Consider, for example, what the task flow for the first-time use of the product would look like. The sequence sketched in Figure 5.8 shows the steps a user might follow to create a recipe, edit the recipe details, browse the book, or select a recipe card to cook from.

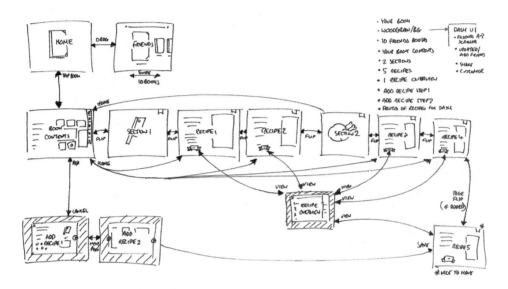

Figure 5.8. Sketching out the sequence of screens

And here are some tips for success:

■ Start to notice sequencing for the products you use in your day-to-day life.

■ Refer again to the scenarios of use for your product and consider at a big-picture level the links between steps in a process, and where the user will need to traverse.

■ Aim to make the path from A to B seamless. Think about where the user comes from (for example, a Google search), and where they might be going (they could be looking for your business's opening hours on your website). Consider making steps as short as they can possibly be (place your opening hours on the home page instead of the contact page).

■ Sketch out the linkage between screens and think about whether arriving at these different locations within your product out of context would make sense to the user.

■ Think about the steps you can eliminate and try drawing your sequence without them; then walk a potential user through your sequence.

Microdetails

Microdetails result in the little "wow" moments that make a huge difference to product designs. They are the tiny features of a design that might be overlooked or thought of as insignificant, but which ultimately show the amazing thought, care, and consideration that has gone into the design at each and every level.

The sum of a series of small experiences within a product is what makes or breaks it; when done well, they stand out to users. A focus on microdetails tells users that their needs have been considered to a minute level, making their experience with the product pleasurable.

For example, consider the way Path[5] shows you what time messages were posted as you scroll, or the pull-down refresh that is now standard for many iPhone apps. These are little "wow" moments in interaction design that really indicate an emotional connection with users.

Microdetails are starting to be a huge differentiator in product design. They are often what users remember long after their interaction with the product is finished, as they tend to communicate personality and shape individual appeal for one product over another. Consider the spring-back nav sketched in Figure 5.9.

---

[5] https://path.com/

Figure 5.9. The small stuff that makes a big difference

Here are some further tips for success:

- Ponder over your entire product and what aspects of the design will be regularly used. Consider what will trigger the need to use these design features.

- Think about inputs, user feedback for a given action, instructions to aid understanding, and different product states that can be communicated in creative ways.

- Contemplate the interactions attached to these features and ask, "What are the microdetails that will make the overall interaction a pleasure? What will help convey personality? What might go unnoticed, but if noticed will make a difference?"

- Consider what might bring out a positive emotional response in your users and thereby increase their engagement with your product. Remember, microdetails aren't vital to your product functioning, but show users that you understand their needs and care enough to bother.

▓ Avoid overdoing it—microdetails are most noticeable when there are only two or three strong "wow" moments to observe within a product. Too many and you can tip the balance to looking like you've tried too hard. Be careful!

The only thing better than sketching on your own is to sketch your ideas with others on your team or your client, so let's explore how you might do that now.

Sketching with Others

Ultimately, sketching is the best way to form a shared understanding with others. Invite potential users, your client (including their consultants and contractors), or your team (if you have one) to discuss designs, and watch ideas multiply.

Discussing with others what you've seen and heard and what you are thinking helps ideas to mature. By focusing on the fundamentals, and avoiding discussions of gradients, colors, and textures, you're able to cement what is required.

The aim of sketching with others is to:

▓ review a range of design ideas
▓ be willing to learn something new
▓ challenge your own thinking and reframe the design problem
▓ critique ideas and decide as a consensus the areas of focus
▓ rapidly generate more ideas
▓ allow the best ideas to progress

For a session to be useful, you need to have a clear plan for what you want to achieve, as well as a set way to approach design problems.

Come Together to Critique Designs

When you have everyone in the room as seen in Figure 5.10—whether it's your team, your client, or stakeholders from a range of broader business areas—you'll need some structure for how to conduct things. As with any collaborative activity in the UX process, you can assume your trusty tools of the trade will be required in large amounts (A3 paper, pens, markers, and sticky-notes) for everyone to use throughout the session.

Figure 5.10. Reviewing designs with others

Once you have the right people and equipment, here are some steps to follow:

▓ Make sure there's someone running the process, moderating comments, and moving the meeting along. This person needs to outline any rules of interaction and communication for the session, and generally keep everyone on track and on time.

▓ Clearly restate the business problem that you're intending to solve, revisit your main users, and then discuss any business drivers or goals.

▓ It helps to review the project vision too, especially if you've been looking at other sites or solutions, as it might color your view or sway you from your original intention.

▓ Review individual designs by putting them up on the wall or windows where everyone can see them.

▪ Allow the mind behind each design the time and space to explain what they were trying to achieve, and let them raise what they like and don't like about their own ideas and concepts.

▪ Think before you react. Ask people to elaborate on the areas that are unclear to you, using questions that are positive and inquisitive. Remember there is no right or wrong at this stage, so be considerate and don't criticize.

In a great speech by Jonathan Ive on Steve Jobs at the "Celebrating Steve" event,[6] he discusses the "fragility of ideas" and puts it best:

> "Steve used to say to me—and he used to say this a lot—'Hey Jony, here's a dopey idea.'
>
> And sometimes they were. Really dopey. Sometimes they were truly dreadful. But sometimes they took the air from the room and they left us both completely silent. Bold, crazy, magnificent ideas. Or quiet simple ones, which in their subtlety, their detail, they were utterly profound.
>
> And just as Steve loved ideas, and loved making stuff, he treated the process of creativity with a rare and a wonderful reverence. You see, I think he better than anyone understood that while ideas ultimately can be so powerful, they begin as fragile, barely formed thoughts, so easily missed, so easily compromised, so easily just squished."

This is an amazing truth—ideas are easily missed. They can be overlooked or squashed during even the best design processes, so be careful at this early stage you are not the one to tread on some great ones.

Collaborate to Nut Out a Design Problem

Distinct from purely critiquing each other's designs, collaboratively sketching solutions to a specific design problem is great for generating new ideas on how to solve a particularly hairy issue that you may be facing.

---

[6] http://tech.fortune.cnn.com/2011/10/24/jonathan-ive-on-steve-jobs-and-the-fragility-of-ideas

Use your scenarios as viewed through a particular persona to guide you, or pick out a single screen and ask everyone to design how they think it should appear in a limited amount of time (say, only ten minutes). You may wish to select the most important screen in your product. This process is ideal for extracting ideas from people who might not ordinarily be designers, as well as possible design directions that failed to be realized at an individual level.

Here are some steps to follow:

- Run a quick sketch activity to generate ideas around the given feature or page of your product that needs solving (for example, dashboard, landing page, recipe page, and so on). The aim is to generate as many ideas as possible.

- Review these designs by having everyone to present their design directions back to the group. During this process, call out questions and collaborate to arrive at the best ideas.

- Run the next cycle of sketches to iterate on the design concepts once again. You'll find that the most popular ideas start appearing in the revised solutions.

Who decides the right way to go?

Ideally, the agreed design direction should be the result of a collaborative effort; failing this, you need to rely on the person leading the design project to move everyone forward, as in Figure 5.11.

There are bound to be times when you're unsure of the right solution—and these are the times to consider inviting your users into the process again, as a way to sense-check your assumptions and approach.

Figure 5.11. Agree on the design direction

Musing on How Your Users Think

There are many preset patterns or metaphors in day-to-day life that you can draw on in your design work to help you understand how people might expect your product to function. Arguably, the best designs are those that are so close to users' expectations that they immediately understand—or mentally decode—how to interact with them.

That said, strict adherence to metaphors from the physical world can make your design look unnecessarily dated, or awkward and overly busy. Furthermore, it can distract from the overall experience if the user needs to interpret it.

A contentious topic lately is **skeuomorphism**, which refers to design elements that deliberately make new objects look older and more familiar, leaning heavily on realism. Generally, the issue is where the design feature offers little or no purpose, taking mimicry to a whole new (and often unnecessary) level. Figure 5.12 shows an example of this, although stitching patterns have become a trend on their own.

Occasionally, it will have the opposite effect to the one intended if the users are unfamiliar with the original concept. If they are new to an industry, for example, they may fail to understand the design features based on real-world objects they've never used.

As designers, it is our job to understand and plug into the mental frameworks users already have in place, where relevant, so that we can design solutions that are recognizable and intuitive. We should look at mimicking the old to demonstrate how the interface operates where there is a relevant real-world reference, but avoid laying it on unnecessarily.

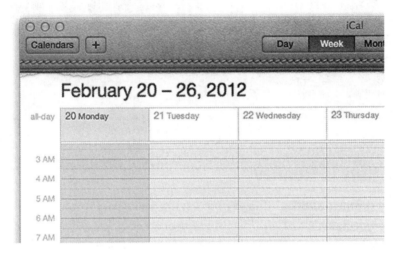

Figure 5.12. Getting stitched up: the jury is out

The recent rise of ebooks has seen the bookshelf metaphor widely adopted to demonstrate the space to store books electronically. When we see this example, we know how it will work: when we buy a book, it will appear on our digital bookshelf. Figure 5.13 compares a real-world example with its digital offshoot.

Figure 5.13. Physical and digital bookshelves

Perception Is Reality

A common design problem is the gap between a user's perception of how a product works and a designer's assumptions of the user's knowledge, given their level of familiarity with it. We refer to the user's perception of how a product works as the **mental model**.

As suggested, what users understand of a product or service may not necessarily be based on fact. In this regard, user perception is reality, and in the absence of a clear design pattern or model to follow, they'll assign their assumed reality to help them make sense of and understand the way it works.

Identifying where we have assumed too much knowledge on the part of our users is one of the main reasons for evaluating and testing a working model of our designs. When you try something new in your designs, think carefully about how you'll assist users to construct a clear mental model of it.

Using Metaphor to Communicate Intent

Consider the rise of tasks we might perform in the offline world being digitized so that we may do them, in a metaphorical sense, online, such as Pinterest.[7]

Pinterest is a digital version of the popular offline activity of creating mood boards or inspiration boards out of bits of paper, cloth, or words that you might find in magazines. Like the offline activity, you find inspirational images (from across the Web) and then "pin" them to your own digital mood board.

When people came to Pinterest for the first time, they didn't require instructions up front, even though it was a new service. It built on concepts that users were already aware of, and the design cleverly plugs into these mental models and extends them logically to the digital world. Compare the old-school mood board with Pinterest in Figure 5.14.

Figure 5.14. Pinning up images on inspiration boards

Pinterest makes setting up and "pinning" items from across the Web dead easy for the user. Simplicity is the secret sauce in behavior design, and a principle that we discussed in Chapter 4 as being essential to the overall success of a product.

---

[7] http://pinterest.com/

Patterns of Everyday Life

Take a moment to stop and think about some common design patterns that users easily recognize. What have you used previously in your design work that was successful? Was there ever a time you strayed from the norm and observed poor results?

Using Social Media to Ask Questions

You can—and should—involve your users several times through your design process, and the concept phase is no exception; however, exactly when you do this will depend on the design solutions you are putting forward and whether you need fresh eyes to help you work through or brainstorm a problem.

Be creative in how you engage your users during this stage. I find it's useful is to draw on social media—such as Yammer or Facebook (seen in Figure 5.15)—to set up a closed research group to discuss issues during the design process.

Select a group of users you might have met via your research phase, or expand on this group through other channels (perhaps via your client, a recruitment agent, or other social media channels).

Having such a forum allows for rapid feedback to all manner of questions, including those concerning actual designs. It also generates conversation around the topic, giving us more insight into the way our users think and behave. For example, when we were designing our recipe app, discussion centered on cooking and meal preparation, finding inspiration, and, of course, recipe organization.

Going to your users early and often ensures you'll always discover some new information that positively impacts your design work.

Figure 5.15. Communicating with your potential users

Here are some further tips:

- Monitor the group regularly and post questions or observations from day-to-day life that might relate to the topic of interest.

- Present your sketches by explaining how the design will work so that people can understand the context. Gauge their response and talk through the good and bad as they see it.

- Ask your users to consider several items; for example, issues about page layout might also raise questions of labeling and categorization, so be sure to ask for all the details you need.

- Be ready to move with the flow of the conversation and adapt to what happens with the group (that is, improvise as required).

Case Study: Designing a Recipe App

When we started sketching, we explored several ways of managing and storing recipes. The design pattern we kept returning to—individually, and as a group—was a digital recipe book.

Initially, we scanned the app store to see what was available in the marketplace at the time. As the research and concept phases progressed, we continued to monitor newly launched apps and explore design patterns for our situation.

This helped to set the scene on a few levels; we were able to see what might compete with our product, as well as explore various design patterns used in apps that were not cooking- or recipe-focused (that is, focus on parallel industries).

As we explored, we asked ourselves:

- What is currently available in the cooking and recipe space?

- Are there any apps performing the same task?

- How are people managing recipes in the real world?

- What metaphors can we carry across from parallel offerings in day-to-day life?

- What common design patterns will allow us to deliver a "book"?

- What else? (As we were yet to reach the stage of fixing our design direction, we were better off exploring some more.)

A Place to Be Inspired

As part of our process, we printed screenshots of competing apps and placed them on the wall, as you can see in Figure 5.16. This meant we could refer to them when we came together as a group, or when we needed to articulate our project to anyone new.

So what were some of the things we found that had a profound impact on how we visualized the future design?

Figure 5.16. Looking for inspiration from advertising

Our initial vision was inspired by recording cherished family recipes, so some of our design inspiration drew on vintage food advertising and cookbooks, such as the samples in Figure 5.17. This visual theme resonated with us, so at this early stage an initial design direction was born.

Vintage cookery books

Figure 5.17. Looking for inspiration from old books

We cross-referenced old styles with new ones that were intending to look old or be inspired by a vintage feel. Looking and comparing these with new design styles across the cooking industry (books, advertising, and even websites and apps) confirmed for us what we *didn't* want the app to look like. Figure 5.18 shows our visual library of design resources.

Figure 5.18. The visual look and feel that matched our vision

Apart from the look, we investigated the types of interactions we wanted to achieve, and found them in a range of parallel industry offerings. Looking outside of what was being done in the recipe space alerted us to simple and intuitive design patterns that related to a book metaphor. Parallel patterns we looked to included scrapbooks, diaries, and journals, newspaper or news aggregator apps, and organizers.

Thinking about Cooks

At the start of our project, we wanted to be mindful of the different types of users that might be interested in the concept. We searched the Web for lots of images that captured the vibe of a given segment and collated what I'd call a segment assumption (like partially formed personas). This helped to trigger early discussions about segments we thought would use the app, as Figure 5.19 demonstrates, and the considerations in light of this.

Figure 5.19. Segment assumptions keep us focused from the beginning

Figure 5.20 was created as a quick reference point for the design team, before we had even started the research stage process. These assumptions were basically just a visualization of our recruitment outline (discussed in Chapter 3). Once research was completed, I created a few primary personas. These were based on merging what I'd seen in our research efforts and secondary research conducted on the Web (that is, research papers, articles, news items, and so on).

Figure 5.20. Detailed personas help to narrow our focus

The message here is that you need to create documents for your project that work for the different stages you're at. You need to start forming a framework of your users before your research is complete, and use this as you talk about your product or service with other stakeholders on your team.

Documents that help remind you of your end-users at all stages are worth pursuing; however, you need to do what makes sense for your project, so invest as much or as little time in them as makes sense.

Considering the First-time Use of the App

You can go to great detail describing different situations or contexts, but if you're stuck, start where a user encounters the service for the first time. Let's explore the first-time use of our cooking app.

Example 5.1. First-time use scenario

"Darci is chatting to her best friend, Blake, on the phone about what they cooked on the weekend. They start talking about a new app that lets you create and store recipes to share with close friends and family. Darci decides to purchase the app and goes to the app store to check it out."

The key tasks in this process will be:

1. visit the app store
2. purchase the cooking app
3. start using the app

This scenario led to lots of thinking around the overall user experience the first time they were exposed to the app. A series of sketches was created to discuss with the wider team, in which I envisaged how the first-time experience could work.

Placing the user at the center of the design helped to remind me of how the product would be used. It allowed me to come up with an experience that was unique and would have an impact, right from the minute they downloaded the app and started using it.

This process also helped to identify design gaps and little details within the design that we believed would make the product stand out. Additionally, it was in line with the original experience we wanted to deliver.

Going to Our Users Again

We started another Yammer group that invited people from the research phase of our process, as well as recruiting new people via special interest groups and broader networks (for example, professional food writers or cooks).

This group was a great source of more focused feedback to questions about general usage. For example, would they bother writing recipe information into a digital format? How did they record and store recipe information?

This assisted us in answering questions around the categorization of content and the use or existence of a special recipe book.

Sketching Ideas on Our Own

The app team started sketching individually and then came together as a group. No matter what our background was, we all sketched. That meant that the designers, the developer, and the researchers all tucked in and demonstrated how we visualized the design solution.

There were many and varied results from our sketching efforts; some team members (being designers) produced thoughtful sketches to imagine the linkages and metaphors we were exploring, as seen in Figure 5.21. Others explored first-time use and tried to consider sequencing and the overall experience.

All approaches were valid, and generated lengthy discussion around the design problem we were trying to solve.

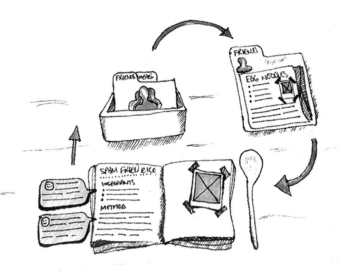

Figure 5.21. Sketching ideas: some artistic examples

Sketching and Workshops with the Team

Once we'd thought through the interactions enough on our own, we came together to critique everyone's ideas.

Some of the initial questions raised based on the review of the first-time use scenario included:

- Should we do a wizard-style step-through of the first-time use experience, or should we let the users do the bare minimum to start using the app, and then explore their new recipe book themselves?

- What experience do we want to deliver: a locked and bounded app, or a more open and exploratory one?

- How will users feel coming to the app and having an empty book with no friends or content?

- Should we offer a team book that allows us to put in recipes from featured chefs or cafés?

- Should we put a few recipes in the users' book that they can then remove if preferred?

How many book covers and styles should we offer to users?

Should we offer different page types and textures for users to customize their book with?

Should we allow users to upload a photo of themselves or family members for the book cover?

How difficult might ordering a printed book from the app be if we allow too much customization of the cover and internal pages?

Should we limit choice so that printing is manageable and cost-effective?

As you can see, the sketching process raised many questions, with the group sessions helping us refocus on the bigger-picture offering that we hoped to deliver.

Collaborative Design Sessions

Collaboratively sketching in ten-minute cycles helped generate ideas for how specific areas of the app might work, such as the recipe pages and main landing pages.

This process also aided us in arriving at our preferred designs, as we started to see the same patterns coming up time and again. It also provided a lot of laughs, as shown in Figure 5.22.

The dominant design metaphors for us at that time were a recipe book that emulated a real-world, treasured family recipe scrapbook, and an index card box of recipes.

Figure 5.22. Collaborating to sketch and keeping it friendly!

The process enabled us to list the features we needed so that we could finalize the core of the design and its interactions. We'd then move into creating an interactive model of our designs to see if the framework would behave as we expected.

This helped clarify what could be achieved in the time frame we had originally set. Like many projects, our timelines were blowing out, and what started quite naively as a six-week project was now more like 20 weeks.

At the start of the concept phase, we had weekly design workshops to discuss all manner of design ideas and problems; as the project progressed, we started daily stand-up meetings as well as weekly design showcases on a Friday afternoon.

This approach was really useful for design decisions we needed to make, so make sure you try it out on your own project work.

What was this product shaping up to be?

Our ultimate goal was starting to take shape: to create a digital recipe book that could be shared with friends and family, that had an important link to the physical world.

We envisaged that users would invite friends via Facebook, as is standard for most social media-based apps. The app would then need to allow friends to view each other's books and swap recipes within the app itself.

Handling the social aspect of the app was a design challenge that we spent a lot of time workshopping and debating. How would the user view notifications, comment on friends' books, or comment on a single recipe? Would there be a consolidated view of activity at the front of their book for everyone, or would each book hold unique activity related to that book?

Another design challenge was how to handle customization of a digital book, particularly in allowing users to order their book as a physical book, or gift the book to others. We believed the link to the physical world would be key to encouraging users to create content in the digital space, and round out an entire experience; however, managing that goal and thinking about flexibility with the design was tricky.

Ultimately, group conversations helped keep our energy up and remind us of our core vision and broader experience goals.

Draw Together

We've introduced the idea of sketching as early as possible to generate many approaches to your design problem, funneling down to a few options as you progress. Sketching—on our own or collaboratively—saves time and money, and brings others into the design process.

We also looked at some techniques to explore interactions your users might have with your product, and discussed some approaches for keeping the voice of the user loud and clear while you design—through the use of personas, scenarios, and social media groups that allow you to engage with your users quickly and easily.

In Chapter 6, we'll focus on firming up our interaction design approach. We'll apply the visual layer and prototype the solution we're heading towards, in order to refine our approach through further user validation. We'll also start to see the interaction design model for the recipe app come to life. It's an exciting stage!

Recap of What You Need to Know

- Sketching to help you think:

  - Avoid letting your fear of drawing stop you from sketching to solve design problems.

  - Create stories and narratives that help you imagine the user in your design process.

  - Think through the eyes of your personas and consider "What would they do?"

  - Use scenarios as a design tool to bring your personas to life and explore the interaction design of your product.

  - Use the storyboarding technique to explore the overall experience you want to deliver.

  - Explore interactions that are relevant to your design problem.

  - Be inspired by what else is out there.

  - Scan for patterns that work from parallel and related fields.

  - Generate lots of ideas before you focus on the ones to take forward and prototype.

- Sketching with others:

  - Invite others into your process to share ideas and align thinking.

  - Critique sketches, but remember there are no wrong approaches.

  - Collaborate and sketch out design solutions in a workshop environment with your colleagues.

  - Make sure you don't tread on any great ideas before they get the chance to go further!

- Thinking about how your users think:

- Draw upon useful metaphors or patterns that are well known.

- Understand the user's mental model of your product.

- Add your ideas of the user's mental model to a wall in your project room for inspiration.

- Set up a social media group to keep a dialogue going with your users throughout your design process.

- Consider running design workshops that draw on users, your client, and team members to help to check your approach to design early and often.

Where to next? Let's prototype the solution!

6

Prototype the Solution

In Chapter 5, we discussed sketching as a way to help expand your understanding of the design challenge you face. By generating lots of ideas on paper—by yourself, and with your team—you're in an effective position to explore a range of approaches that might work. The next step is to prototype.

Prototypes are a simulation of your design intent. They provide a clear vision of what needs to be built, and help you to communicate that view to your client.

They raise design problems early, and assist you to understand constraints—because you will indeed hit these at some point. They'll aid you in reaching an alternative solution early in the project life cycle, long before code is formalized and it all becomes too late.

Prototypes are an essential tool in the UX toolbox, and in this chapter we'll cover: using them as demos to encourage buy-in to your ideas; learning from prototypes and confirming user requirements; and why your prototypes should be hacked together.

We Are Still in the Concept Phase

Because we're still in the concept phase of our UX process, shown in Figure 6.1, we're still understanding the design problem and exploring possible solutions.

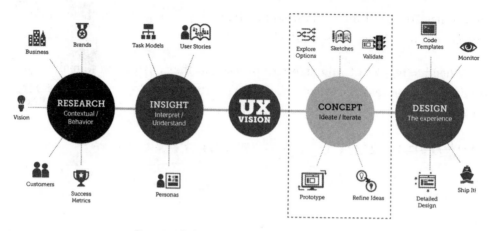

Figure 6.1. Concept phase: prototype the interactions

Sketching is the first step towards prototyping; you can think of it as the lightweight version of establishing your design story so that you can simulate it to ensure you're headed in the right direction.

Sketches alone are not enough to explore potential scenarios of use for your design; nor are they enough to sell an idea to your team or client. At this stage, you're validating your ideas and thinking through the design problem; prototyping the design will help you to focus on the sequencing, flow, and microdetails of your product that will deliver the "wow" moments.

Prototypes are a perfect vehicle for canvassing feedback on the design, and the various interactions from your users too … but we'll cover iterative testing and refinement of your prototypes in Chapter 7. For now, we'll focus on developing the prototype, and consider internal feedback and discussion.

Selling the Dream

A **prototype** is essentially a proof of concept for your design ideas as they stand right now. I like to think of them as a great way to showcase your vision for the end design as it evolves.

As we've previously established, you are not your user, and failing to understand this will result in a design gap. Prototyping identifies user requirements and assists in defining the product's scope. This allows you and your client to manage risk and ensure there are no nasty surprises at the end of the project when it is all too late.

Prototypes are the ultimate platform for showing your client "This is what I'm thinking from a design perspective."

They need to be part of your standard process, as they enable you to make your product concept real and tangible before it's actually developed. This is essential for identifying issues in your design work, and then refining and perfecting them.

Prototypes: Part of an Iterative Process

Prototypes, much like sketching, are fairly standard deliverables throughout any proper UX process. They are about filling in the details and allowing the concept to be experienced, even if only at a rudimentary level. Lines scribbled on paper are an essential part of the thinking process when it comes to design, but they only get you so far.

Dynamic interactions need to be experienced so that we may understand the linkages between states. Prototyping makes you focus on the detail involved in a given task. This focus means it is harder to brush over supporting screens or in-between steps; you must address them to make the model work.

Once you've simulated the experience, you can try it out with your users and see what happens when a working model of your design is in their hands. The process permits you to focus on the microdetails that will make a big difference, allowing you to continue cycling through iterations of testing with users till you reach the desired result.

In this way, the prototype shines a light on what it feels like to use your design, and allows you to reflect on whether there are too many steps, understand if your process flows well, and, most importantly, enables you to determine if others understand it. Figure 6.2 demonstrates where prototypes fit within the iterative testing cycle of a UX process.

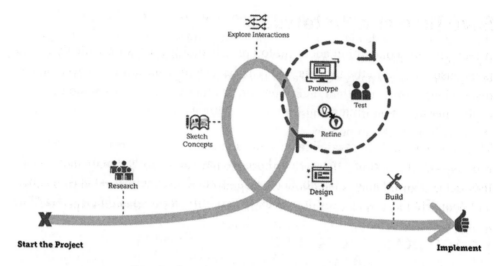

Figure 6.2. Prototypes facilitate an iterative testing cycle

The Main Reasons to Prototype

Prototypes inspire participation from others in the design process. They can take many forms, but they are all constructed quickly to answer critical questions about the design in order to move forward.

In summary, the main reasons to use prototypes in your design work are to:

- simulate the overall experience and generate more design ideas

- communicate what you intend with the design to others (such as your client or team)

- validate the experience with real users of the system, helping you refine your approach and identify issues before formal coding begins

- manage and clearly define the scope of your design work, taking into consideration estimates of development work

- offer a vision of the design's final state

Prototypes give you and your client an opportunity to test the waters, rather than learn too late that your design will fail.

Save Time and Prototype

A recurring misconception about prototyping is that it wastes valuable time, and is inconsequential to the process. This can be a significant hurdle to overcome in discussions with your client, management, or other team members who've never experienced the benefit it brings.

There are so many tools available nowadays that allow you to create working digital prototypes, all at a speed that was impossible ten years ago. Software tools such as Balsamiq,[1] Axure,[2] and iRise[3] allow you to grab elements, drop them on your canvas, and instantly have the look and behaviors that will allow others to experience the design before you commit to a coded implementation.

By taking the time to prototype, many design problems can be properly resolved in your sketching process, instead of rearing their ugly heads when the system is already implemented. This latter scenario is best avoided, as it can compromise the quality of the decisions made as you rush to develop the final solution.

 Experience Interactive Prototyping

Have you ever created an interactive prototype? If so, what was the experience like? What would you do differently next time? If not, what are some barriers that have prevented you from making one?

Prototype to Learn

Speed and agility are great assets in a design team. They give you the ability to create working models of a design that you can then iterate quickly and frequently. The ideas and lessons associated with creating a simulated model of your design are invaluable. The more critical the functions to your service, and the more complex the design issue, the more useful a prototype will be.

---

[1] http://www.balsamiq.com/
[2] http://www.axure.com/
[3] http://www.irise.com/

Where did we leave off after sketching?

During the sketching process, we created storyboards and mapped out a sequence of screens to demonstrate how our app would operate. Figure 6.3 demonstrates our working model.

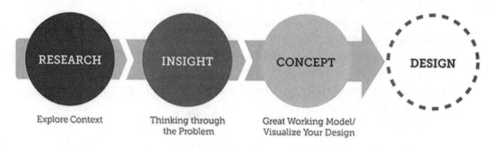

Figure 6.3. Moving through the stages of our process

As you prototype and refine your design, the pieces of the design puzzle start to fit together. You'll then put your prototype in front of potential end-users to ensure your product works as you imagined it. This process assures you that your designs will be understood and therefore accepted by users once launched (we'll cover testing your prototypes in Chapter 7).

Different Types of Prototypes

Prototypes should be quick and basic, gradually increasing in complexity as your ideas mature and your design direction firms up. You can use paper, digital tools, cardboard, foam, video, or storytelling to communicate what a product or service might be to others; the format you select will depend on what you are designing. Figure 6.4 shows the limitations of using paper to display your concepts.

Figure 6.4. You reach a point where paper just isn't enough ...

In addition, prototypes are often referenced as either "low fidelity" or "high fidelity," depending on the degree to which we can view interactions and transitions in the context of our design.

Fidelity Explained

In UX/prototyping, **fidelity** refers to the degree of alignment the prototype has to the end result of the product.

High fidelity (hi-fi) conforms more closely or almost exactly to the end state (a more accurate reproduction); with **low fidelity** (lo-fi) being less accurate in terms of closeness to the desired end result.

We'll now explore some forms of prototyping.

Sketches and Storyboards

There are reasons for and against the degree of fidelity that you choose for prototyping. One reason to keep them lo-fi and rough is that it takes less effort, and you're more able to rapidly change it.

High-fidelity solutions can sometimes be distracting for clients and stakeholders, who can be swayed by colors, typefaces, and imagery, instead of focusing on the arrangement of items on the page. This is one of the biggest arguments for starting out using a lower-fidelity approach, such as the sketch shown in Figure 6.5.

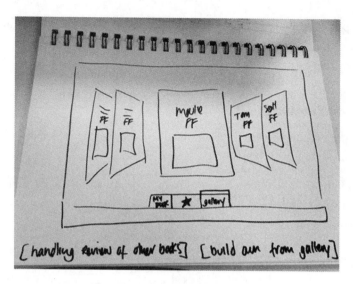

Figure 6.5. Sketching to visualize an idea

Wireframes and Clickable Wireframes

A **wireframe** is a basic skeleton for the design you are creating. It is intended to show structure, information hierarchy, functions, and content, while communicating through the lack of color and polish that it is still very much a work-in-progress. Its main purpose lies in helping you to better realize the functionality, behaviors, and content you need for different areas of your design.

Creating wireframes is the first step towards understanding the transitions between states in your design, and they are a great way to progress your problem-solving beyond sketching. Consider how our sketches in Figure 6.5 have developed into wireframes in Figure 6.6.

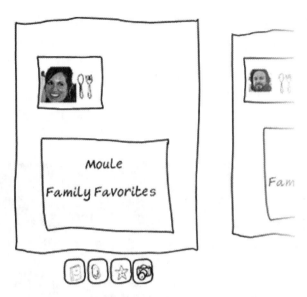

Figure 6.6. Wireframes: another level of understanding

This example was done in PowerPoint, a reasonably lo-fi tool, yet a really quick-and-dirty way to communicate the overall interactions envisaged for a range of scenarios across the recipe app.

PowerPoint and Keynote are similar useful tools that allow you to create "clickable" wireframes where you can click through screens, giving the impression of interactivity that sketching or static wireframes alone cannot offer.

Interactive Prototypes

When it comes to user-testing your product, your prototypes should ideally simulate the experience of using your product in a much more realistic manner than sketches. Personally, I've found that hi-fi prototypes result in more useful feedback from user tests of digital products. People are unable to visualize the final product when it doesn't look real.

For this reason, we always present our visual designs (rather than interaction designs) as hi-fi prototypes for user-based testing.

Basic wireframes are great for exploring the arrangement of features on a page, as well as how the overall sequencing and flow of screens might occur, helping the internal team understand and explore a particular approach quickly. Alternatively, high-fidelity visuals (closer to our expected final designs) with light interactions are best for exploring user reactions.

It is worth reiterating that while these high-fidelity prototypes are often visually rich—such as the one shown in Figure 6.7—they are held together with a series of hotspots (clickable areas), shortcuts, sticky tape, and superglue. The aim is to give the illusion of a fully functioning site.

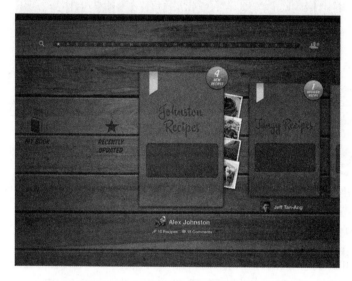

Figure 6.7. Initial design concepts in a high-fidelity prototype

The Case for Low- and High-fidelity Prototypes

Making your design concepts as visually close to the end product as you can identifies problems or issues early in the design cycle; however, it may require more time to develop, delaying the amount of user feedback you can procure. Ensure you focus on the higher end of the fidelity scale as quickly as you can for exploring design concepts, as illustrated in Figure 6.8.

Figure 6.8. Exploring with a more polished design

Think of This Stage as an Experiment

Good prototypes allow you to validate your design ideas at a very low cost to see if they work in practice. Prototyping, in all its forms of fidelity, is a time to experiment and refine your thinking and design direction as indicated in Figure 6.9.

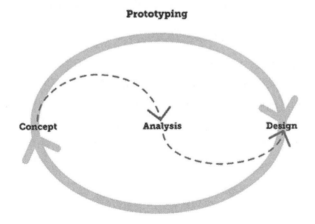

Figure 6.9. Prototype to refine the design direction

Before you start prototyping, think about what it is you want to bring to life in a simulation of a real-world interaction. Then you can evaluate the performance of your design.

Factors Your Prototype Should Address

You can expect your current design to change as it undergoes iterative testing and is refined. You should, however, consider the following before you start prototyping.

What the Core Interactions Are

During research, you should have identified a number of core tasks that your product will need to facilitate for a user to accomplish their mission. A task analysis will guide you in how to support your users through important behavioral patterns or adapting to risky functionality.

For example, we need to support several basic tasks for the recipe app, including:

- inviting or adding friends
- customizing their book
- browsing their friends' books
- adding a recipe to their book
- making a comment on a recipe

Task analyses are easily documented in a spreadsheet or a word document, and help your design team visualize and prioritize the screens to be designed.

Once completed, you're in a better position to consider the links between screens that will underpin your product's structure, often called a task flow. Consider the task flow and relevant screens in Figure 6.10.

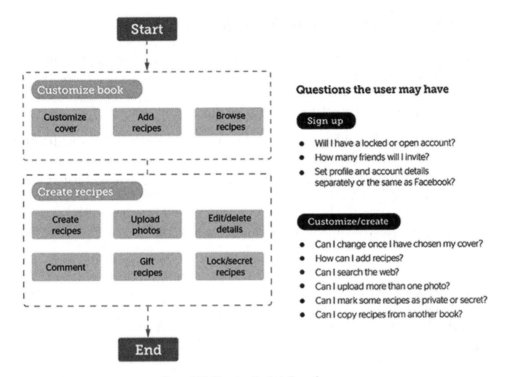

Figure 6.10. Mapping the task flow of screens

Remember in Chapter 5 I spoke of sequencing? Sequencing is the combination of several task flows across your product. We covered how sequencing that is not carefully considered can provide a jarring experience to end-users as they move from one task to another. Hence, it's important to consider as many possible pathways through your product as you can, to prevent your overall product experience from falling flat.

Prototyping helps to bring user pathways through your product to life and aids in the refinement of the sequence of screens required to complete a range of tasks.

Information Structure

Depending on the size and scale of your product, the information and content requirements can vary greatly. For example, the information structure required for a retail or government website, which is usually deep and complex with multifaceted content, will be quite different to the content needs found within an app.

Essentially, **information architecture** (or IA) is the term used to describe the structure of a system, which is the way information is grouped or categorized. IA affects whether the user can actually find what they want within your product.

As always, context of your product and research into the way your users think and behave should drive the creation of initial information structures. The most effective information and content models reflect the way people think about the subject matter.

A technique to involve users in the creation of site IA or sitemaps is to conduct a card-sort activity. This activity allows you to understand how users think about, cluster, and group information into categories, enabling you to come up with a draft model of your IA.

 Getting Sorted

A **card-sort activity** has users sorting a series of cards—each labeled with a piece of content or functionality—into groupings that make sense to them. It's useful to conduct in a workshop setting or at the start or end of user-testing; it can even be done online using various tools (see Optimal Sort[4] or Tree Jack,[5] for example).

As with other processes, don't expect to get your IA right on the first go. You'll need to use other methods to help you validate it.

I'm a fan of validating IA structures within the context of a working model, such as a prototype, for the best outcomes. This is because prototypes give users a broader context for understanding where content will sit within the product, and allows you to test task completion within that context. If users struggle to locate what you are asking them to find within your prototype, you need to review your approach.

Figure 6.11 shows a potential interface wireframe for our recipe app, with an initial idea of how recipes may be organized.

---

[4] http://www.optimalworkshop.com/optimalsort.htm
[5] http://www.optimalworkshop.com/treejack.htm

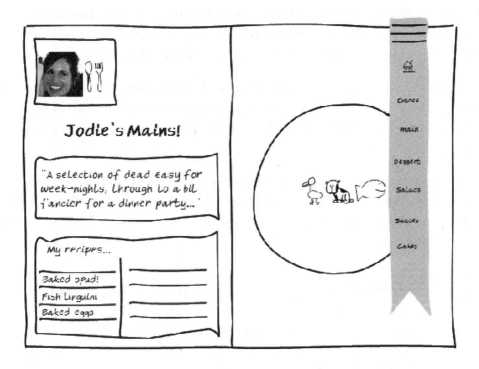

Figure 6.11. Wireframe of one possible solution

In the case of an app, the information structure is quite simple; however, we did hit some questions that need validating with our users in testing.

This list shows the different recipe categorization models we could offer for the app:

- Course: appetizer; entrée; dessert
- Produce: meat; fish; poultry; vegetables; sugar
- Flavor: sweet; savory
- Mixed: appetizer; entrée; dessert; salad; sauces; cakes
- Other

What we'd need to do is create a draft IA and put it within the context of our interactive prototype; then we'd test it with users, for what approach would work best. For example, we could have tested the interface shown in Figure 6.12.

Figure 6.12. Possible interface prototype for testing

Simulate the Experience Using Scenarios

Prototyping should set the scene for the type of experience you are trying to deliver with your product. The human experience is brought to life through scenarios of use that help to define the extent of the design work needed.

Envisaging an experience based in the user's world makes you consider how you'll create your prototype from the user's perspective, rather than in terms of feature sets.

For example, rather than just thinking of "notifications," we might look to create an experience that sets the context for why notifications will be needed:

Example 6.1. Consider yourself told

While you're on the sofa watching TV, you receive a notification that someone has added one of your recipes to their book. You open the app to see what recipe was copied and who it was. It's Fleur, and she has added your fish linguini, so you send her a quick message to say "Enjoy!"

Putting yourself in the user's shoes allows you to consider the right amount of detail you should put into your design work when you create a prototype. You need to have just enough detail in your scenario so that the user can complete a task; however, it's unnecessary to have all pages realized. We'll look at some examples of scenarios later in the section called "Visualizing Task Flows and Scenarios".

Defining the Scope of the Prototype

Prototyping using scenarios also offers a logical way to limit the scope of your initial design efforts. The point of the prototype is to design a few critical sections within the product, instead of the entire product.

For example, you may limit the amount you are going to prototype by focusing on four to six scenarios that cover a good proportion of your product. Scenarios help you walk through an entire end-to-end user situation without detailing the whole solution or dictating the steps; this frees you up to test your ideas and change direction quickly, and lightens the load on creating the prototype.

There's no need to design everything right now, nor have it fully functioning. Wherever possible, create the illusion of interaction.

 Best-case Scenario

Go back to some of the scenarios created to guide our sketching efforts. Think about how you will expand on these to make them useful as the basis of an app prototype.

When to Resort to Cowboy Coding

Like the designs themselves, high-fidelity prototypes are not supposed to be the foundation code for the final solution; they are just ideas for the final solution.

This is a significant point, because at this stage you won't know if you'll be reusing certain elements or design patterns. In fact, you'll be quite unsure if a certain design direction will actually work when put into practice.

Use whatever tool that allows you to move quickly, and be ready to throw your prototype away. If you do decide to build your prototype using code, now isn't the time to be concerned with writing best-practice, maintainable code; it's okay to use dirty code and hack together whatever works.

You might reuse some of this code later, but don't set out with the mindset that this will be the case. Doing so will waste time and effort, turning what could be done in a day into a task that could take weeks.

Aim to start with an easy-to-manipulate mess and once you establish a direction, start extracting and organizing, sorting, and perfecting.

Remember, "rapid and disposable" should be your mantra when prototyping.

Why do we throw it out?

I mentioned that prototypes should be built quickly and then discarded. This is because the prototype you first create is likely to be very different from the refined approach you end up with a month before you launch your product.

Why? Because we're still solving the design problem, and the act of prototyping actually helps us to solve the design problems we face. As our thinking changes, so do the designs—and therefore the prototype.

The Past is a Foreign Country

Go back and look at some of your old work examples from a year or two ago. How do you feel now when you look at these designs or sketches? Would you approach it differently if given the chance again?

Simulate It, Don't Overbake It!

Creating a prototype need not be a time-consuming process, but it should at least have had enough attention in order to progress logically.

You can move forward with more than one design, too. If you have time, and you or your client want to explore options, you can always prototype several solutions to help you decide what approach best fulfills your project needs.

Try to access real or anonymized data and content to put into your prototypes rather than filler text such as lorem ipsum. Real data and content will help you test all aspects of your product more thoroughly, and identify content layout issues that might occur with your proposed design. It will also help highlight whether content is readable, even identify whether the tone of voice resonates with users. All this is useful to learn and plan for earlier rather than later.

Attempting to break the design model with what might represent real-world information is an ideal way to test how robust and scalable your design will be over time. I've seen many prototypes look great for testing, with beautifully presented information, but sadly fall apart once real data has been added. (We'll talk more about this in Chapter 7 in the context of our case study.)

The ability to input real information will often depend on the nature of your product, as well as what your client can supply. If your client is unable to provide anything for you, you'll need to consider the time/pay-off balance to maintain. You may want to opt for Not Lorem Ipsum.[6]

As you cycle through various iterations of the prototype and update your design, try to experiment with different scenarios that might represent edge cases. These will really test the robustness of your design model and provide a broader coverage of your product and its potential features and functions.

Time well-spent now will help ease any uncertainty you may have when it comes time to go live.

Tools for Your Consideration

In the digital space, there are many online tools that allow you to rapidly construct working models of your design work.

For designing in the browser, there are lots of toolkits, plugins, and libraries online (for example, JavaScript libraries like jQuery UI[7]) that help to extend the average designer's capabilities while keeping the act of prototyping simple. There are no set rules about what is best. Choose what you prefer to use or are most comfortable with.

These resources are making it easier than ever for noncoders to try their hand at a range of simple interactions that help bring their designs to life. As stated, it doesn't

---

[6] http://notloremipsum.com/
[7] http://jqueryui.com/

have to be production–quality code, as long as it demonstrates the intended interactions to your client, users, or team.

Some examples I have encountered include PowerPoint, Keynote, Axure, Balsamiq,
iRise, Visio,[8] Omnigraffle,[9] iMockups,[10] SketchyPad,[11] and HTML and CSS.

Keep reminding yourself that you make a prototype expecting to throw it out; what
you learn is bound to ensure the design approach changes a few times.

Bear in mind it is possible to turn hacky code into something you can actually reuse,
but that should be after several design, test, and refine cycles, and once everyone
is in agreement with the final design direction.

Bringing the Design to Life

Have you ever created an interactive prototype of your design concepts? What
were your experiences? What tools did you use? What did you learn that you'd
do differently next time? If you have not, what would the potential benefits to
your work be?

Mind the Time: Build a Good Prototype

Too often, it's easy to say "we'll cover that off in the build phase." Then, when you
reach this phase and time is tight, important design decisions are rushed, leading
to a mind-set of "just do what is quickest and easiest," rather than focusing on the
best way to solve your design problem.

Make sure you leave enough time for prototyping and experimenting with as many
different pathways through your product as time will allow. Time spent up front
will ultimately save you time later.

Now let's look at how this all translates to our recipe app!

---

[8] http://visio.microsoft.com/
[9] http://www.omnigroup.com/products/omnigraffle/
[10] http://www.endloop.ca/imockups/
[11] http://sketchyapp.com/

Case Study: Designing a Recipe App

As we went deeper into our design process, we moved toward formats that enabled us to view an interactive model of our ideas, once we'd agreed on the general framework we thought would work for the recipe app.

To say we totally moved away from sketching is untrue. In fact, we've continued to use sketching throughout our design process (even at later stages) as a quick way to say "this is what I mean," or "this is what I think it should look like," in our team stand-up sessions and weekly workshops.

Moving from Sketches to Wireframes

I changed to a more interactive model when I had to consider how a few of the key scenarios of use for the app might be played out when transferred from a flat noninteractive view to a simulated model.

I wanted to bring these core interactions to life so that I could click through pages in the workflow, and understand the sequencing needed. This helped to identify areas of the design that required further work. See how our sketches have changed in Figure 6.13.

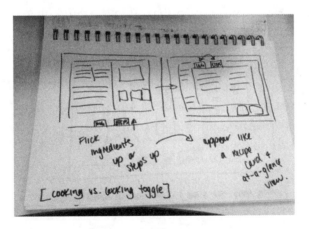

Figure 6.13. Goodbye sketching? Not quite

Many of the design team started using tools that allowed interactions to be modeled at the same time, though they weren't necessarily using the same tool.

What's your tool of choice?

I chose to use PowerPoint for my wireframes. I find it quick and easy to throw ideas onto the page and capture necessary design elements without becoming too hung up on the actual appearance.

For me, this early stage of design concepts must look incomplete and far from fully resolved, and PowerPoint helps you achieve this. This format enabled me to take what I'd learned from the research stage and put it into an interactive context, to be discussed with the wider team.

Not being a visual designer, PowerPoint suits me as it gives the illusion of interaction when in the slideshow mode, clicking between screens to convey a feeling of movement through pages of the app.

As we discussed in the section called "Wireframes and Clickable Wireframes", wireframes are a low-fidelity prototype tool; however, clickable wireframes help to increase the overall fidelity of the format, allowing you to progress your designs as you create a more interactive model.

Figure 6.14 shows my initial wireframe of a recipe page, with a comment from a friend.

Figure 6.14. Unfinished designs still communicate ideas

So what tool did the designers use?

They jumped straight to Photoshop as a preference, using a combination of Photoshop and Keynote to provide the interactions they needed. Photoshop was quicker for them to use, so they felt comfortable putting visuals into place early. They could then work on the visual design based on feedback from the group, maximizing the time they had to refine it before presenting it to users as part of our iterative testing process.

Figure 6.15 shows a designer's take on the same problem using Photoshop.

Figure 6.15. Using tools that allow a bit more polish

Using a few different working models allowed us to nut out design problems as a team, which better prepared us when the time came to involve users to validate our ideas.

Visualizing Task Flows and Scenarios

Prototyping is a way to communicate the intended recipe app interactions, but we needed to define the links between interactions before we could do so.

The core interactions were simple enough to outline. The main features were to create recipes, browse friends' books, and facilitate recipe-swapping and communication.

Figure 6.16 outlines some of the task flows of the app mapped against potential user questions we needed to cover in our scenarios.

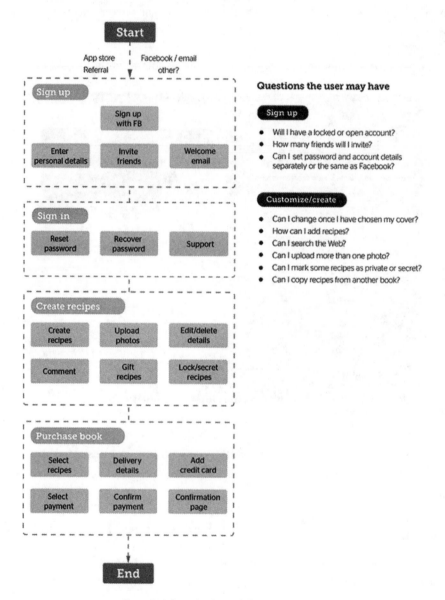

Figure 6.16. Investigating task flows for the app

Creating scenarios would allow us to model the interactions by end-users, and keep the end-user and their needs firmly in our sights. One of the scenarios is shown in Figure 6.17. It also helped us to define the scope of our initial prototype effort.

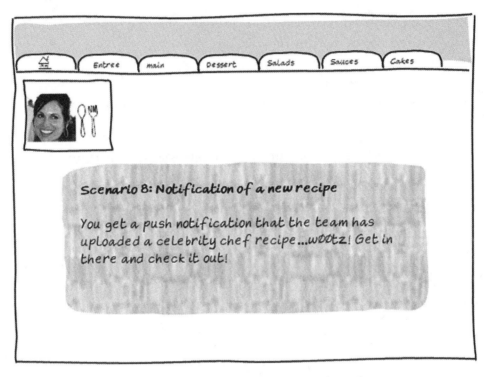

Figure 6.17. Wireframing scenarios helped explore interactions

Some of the scenarios that I initially explored when wireframing included:

- first-time use and initial impressions of the recipe app

- first-time exploration of a user's book (empty book)

- exploration of the team's book (content examples)

- adding friends and browsing their books

- creating a recipe

As we continued exploring the user experience, I expanded on these core scenarios to look more broadly. This helped to imagine features we wanted to deliver as later releases after launching. Some areas of focus included:

- Searching the Web for a recipe to add to their own book

- Requesting a secret recipe (exploring social and secretive elements)

- Receiving notifications that a person has commented on or added one of your recipes

- Entering credit card details and saving them in order to purchase a book

- Gifting their book or parts of their book to a family member (order and purchase a printed version of their book)

When you use a tool that makes wireframing rapid, you can move through a lot of scenarios in a relatively short time frame.

What about the information categories?

We decided to allow users to select from a range of categories so that they could personalize their book. However, we had to limit the number of categories so that the choices would fit comfortably on the navigation ribbon that was part of the design.

In offering a choice, the main problems it presented for us were:

- What if a user wanted to add a recipe from a friend's book to their own, but didn't have the same category?

- What issues would this create if users wanted to then order a printed copy of their book?

We investigated these in user-testing, but in the meantime, we looked at our contextual research data and constructed a model. Refinements to the main information categories would come later.

What were some of the design problems?

The design metaphor for the recipe app was a digital recipe book that allowed users to create, store, and manage recipes. It also enabled a social component that facilitated swapping recipes with friends.

Why a book?

The research showed us that many of the target segments (single foodies and family caterers) had a treasured recipe scrapbook where they recorded recipes from family and friends. We wanted to replicate this book, but digitize it and make it social, like the one shown in Figure 6.18.

The recipe app would enable you to have a recipe book that you could customize and make your own, as well as invite friends with books you could access and browse, so that you could swap recipes.

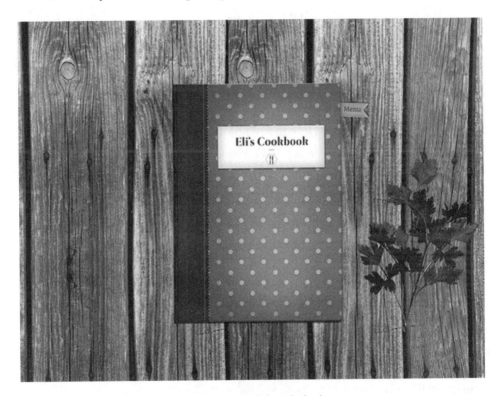

Figure 6.18. It's all about the book

As we started to create interactive models and prepared to test with users, most of our thinking focused on:

First-time use

Should we use a wizard or let users explore? What would the landing page look like when they first created their book?

Creating a recipe

Should we focus on a WYSIWYG editor pattern, where the interface can be switched between editor mode and preview mode, or should users negotiate through two simple screens, different from the main screen, for uploading images and adding recipe details?

A recipe details page   What would be presented on this page and where could they access it from?

The social element   How would we handle the social side of sharing books? How would we present notifications, comments, and new activity within the book?

Customizing the book   How much would we allow users to customize and how many options could we reasonably offer in the first release?

Photos   How many photos would we allow users to upload in the first release?

Categorization   Would we set the categories or allow personalization?

As a team, we went in circles for weeks around this stuff; we had to remind ourselves constantly that this app was all about the book. We therefore decided to do everything we could to reinforce the book metaphor for users as we made design decisions.

We agreed to go into the first round of testing with minimal functionality to test the concept. We'd model the ability to see that users have friends and they have books; facilitate the users' ability to browse their book (that would have dummy content); and create a recipe. None of the interactions would actually work; they'd mainly be images on the screen that a single tap or swipe would activate.

This left many of the design problems for us to test in subsequent iterations, keeping our first round with users as simple as possible so that we could confirm the basic design approach was headed in the right direction. Some of the prototype options are shown in Figure 6.19.

Figure 6.19. Focusing on the options to prototype

Exploring the Interactions in a Hacky Way

Our developers created a high-fidelity prototype in iOS for our first round of user-testing, as opposed to using paper or wireframes.

Not all projects can afford do this, but we gathered it would allow us to experiment with some of the intended interactions of the recipe app, such as the page flip and the movement between books on the main tabletop (the app dashboard).

We wanted the action of pulling open book, and moving between friends' books, to have custom animations themselves, such as the page flip illustrated in Figure 6.20. This needed to be trialled early on, just as we trialled the design, so that we could keep experimenting with the code for the animations (the microdetails of the design).

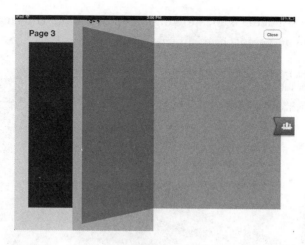

Figure 6.20. Reviewing different interactions for context

For now it was about constructing a clear framework based on our initial designs that would help us bring the animated page-turn features and movement between different recipe books to life. We could then see them working at a basic level for our first round of testing.

Although we had visual designs that indicated the prototype looked finished to the user's eye, in reality they were early, rough designs that we'd continue to refine with each cycle of testing.

We focused our efforts on a basic functional prototype that brought the animated page-turn effects of the app to life. We'd then be able to confirm whether the design approach we'd taken resonated with our end-users.

Interview: Developer's View of the UX Process

From our developer's perspective, prototyping is valuable for experimenting with custom interaction ideas. In the case of this app, there are a few custom transitions that need to be prototyped. At this stage, it was about exploring these in sketch and team meeting sessions, then allowing Jeff (that's our developer) to go back and explore custom animations that might work.

As an example, it was crucial to capture the transition between a user's book and their friends' books. As a team, we wanted a "pulling" sensation that had a sense of resistance before "snapping" between screens. This was discussed but needed to be seen in context of the iPad, allowing experimentation with custom animations from a development perspective, shown in Figure 6.21.

Figure 6.21. The developer's view of the UX process

The second interaction to nail was opening the book, as this needed to transition smoothly from a closed book to a full-screen opened book. For this, our developer had to research various animation techniques and work closely with all the design team to discuss the overall effect. We also had to address any compromises we'd need to make to achieve the desired effect.

Another key interaction requiring prototyping was the "flipping" of book pages. We wanted a page flip that felt effortless (think Flipboard[12]) as opposed to a more literal page curl (think iBooks[13]).

The final interaction we wanted to explore was the navigation ribbon that would be the main way to move between categories within the book. Similar to the move-

---

[12] http://flipboard.com/
[13] http://blog.steventroughtonsmith.com/2010/02/apples-ibooks-dynamic-page-curl.html

ment between the user's book and their friends' books, we wanted the feeling of pulling down on the navigation ribbon to have some resistance and also some bounce to it. Again, this was a custom animation that our developer needed to experiment with to perfect.

I hope this shows the importance of keeping things hacky and imperfect. Until we roughly simulated the experience, we were be unable to understand how many of these animations were going to work together or how they'd actually feel for the user.

In Embryo

At this stage, the prototype was in an embryonic stage and yet to reach the level of development where it could be tested with users. The next two weeks were about bedding down the last of the interaction design, and developing and experimenting with interactions in the iOS prototype in tandem—all to prepare for testing the interactions with our users.

The interactive model helped us solve some of the design problems still being worked through. For example, how to handle notifications and comments, where these placed the user in the book when they received them, the main landing pages, and then the first-time app use scenario.

For now, we were still in the trenches and solving design problems on the fly. I expected this to continue right up until we decided that the design problems were satisfactorily solved, or when we reached deadlines—whatever came first.

Sounds like your typical project, right?

In Chapter 7, we'll explore the iterative testing cycles of a UX process that occurs pre-launch. This is where we'll evaluate the designs we've created in the form of the interactive prototype, and then update the design based on user feedback.

We'll do this three or four times before we finalize our designs and get ready to launch our first release (in Chapter 8).

Recap of What You Need to Know

▨ Selling the dream:

- Simulate the overall experience and generate more design ideas.

- Communicate what you intend with the design to others (your client, your team).

- Validate the experience with real users of the system to help you refine your approach and identify issues before formal coding begins.

- Manage the scope of your design work and clearly define what is in or out of scope for your project.

- Offer a vision of the design's final state for all to agree on.

- Prototype to learn:

  - Learn early (or fail fast)

  - Answer questions and raise new ones

  - Generate new ideas

  - Validate assumptions

  - Compare alternatives

  - Make rapid changes

  - Do hacky stuff for now, aim for an easy-to-manipulate mess that you can establish a direction with, and then worry about organizing, sorting, and perfecting

- Simulate it, don't overbake it!

  - Use tools that you are comfortable with.

  - Throw away your prototypes with ease.

  - Ensure prototypes remind you of the user context.

  - Communicate the right level of detail.

  - Change and update your prototypes frequently.

- Make your prototypes testable for your end-users.

Next up, we run several tests and iterate and repeat user-testing cycles to help in our design refinement process.

Test, Learn, Tweak. Iterate

Throughout the last few chapters, we've spent some time reinforcing the importance of sketching out ideas and transforming them into a working model to bring the design problem you face to life.

A friend of mine once compared prototyping and iterative user-testing to a game of Angry Birds: you aim, fire, watch what happens, and then adjust your approach if you fail to hit the mark. I love this analogy—it really highlights what is intended from a prototype and iterative testing process.

The goal is to learn from what you did wrong, so that you can make it right the next time around. Even the best designers generally don't get it right the first time; you have to learn early and quickly, changing what you do so that you can move on with confidence.

As the clock ticks on your project timeline, it is easy to look for reasons to avoid prototyping and user-testing; however, this process will always save you time and money if you do it early enough. If you don't, and your product fails once launched, you have a big problem. In this chapter, we'll focus on validating the user experience, iterating the solution, and deciding when you're done. As you can see in Figure 7.1, we're still in the concept phase.

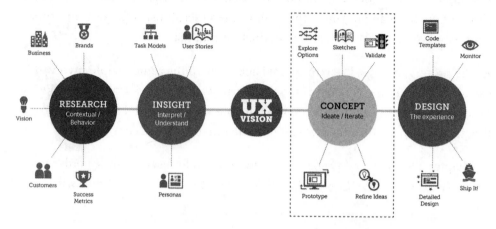

Figure 7.1. Concept phase: iterative testing and refinement

Concept Phase: Iterative Testing

As we discussed in Chapter 5 and Chapter 6, the concept phase is about generating as many plausible solutions as possible; then narrowing your focus on a few that you feel have enough weight to prototype and explore further through interactive models. There is always knowledge to gain from testing your designs with users, and if you want a great product, you have to test early and often.

Iterative means the act of repeating a process with the aim of achieving a desired result. Each repetition of the UX testing process is called an iteration, and the results are used to guide the next testing cycle or iteration.

Validating Our Planned User Experience

Your main focus at this stage should be to learn how to improve the product you have designed. This is done by including users in the process, and although users often feel they're under scrutiny, it is really the design that is being evaluated here.

One factor I've observed from years of prototyping and testing designs is that it *will* fall short of perfect the first time. Trying out your idea on others is the only way to guarantee you'll end up with a better outcome.

Bringing the Users Back

In Chapter 3, I mentioned the importance of having the right people to test, and you should now have an outline of the brief used to recruit users for your up-front contextual research. Well, it's time to dust off that list.

At the prototype stage, I like to invite back some of the same people involved in earlier research. This is to continue the journey as you move from the exploration of ideas and concepts towards a more tangible working model of your design. I do this in addition to introducing new recruits unfamiliar with our designs.

In Chapter 3, we covered preparation and research for user-testing in order to learn about the user's context. Let's adapt those ideas for testing prototypes with users:

- Setting up the environment: Will you be conducting the evaluation in users' homes or offices? In testing labs?

- Recruiting: some of the people you've already seen in earlier research, as well as some new ones.

- Preparing scenarios for your users: These scenarios will have shaped your prototype, and should match the scenarios used to evaluate the success of the design.

- Organizing the format to follow: This includes running a quick pilot to test the flow of your questions and the timing of the session (we'll go over a format you can follow in the section called "Running a Pilot Session to Fine-tune").

- Showing whatever you have ready: Don't be precious about your work being 100% finished—as you iterate, the design will evolve.

- Focusing on a maximum of three or four participants a day: This allows time for discussion with your client or team between and after sessions.

- Listening to what users say during sessions and taking lots of notes: This is so you can refer to your notes later as you discuss outcomes with your team or client.

- Gaining agreement at the end of each day of testing: It's important that the team is all on the same page when it comes to the design features that were validated, and the features that need to be further refined for the next day of testing.

In time, your judgment will become better at assessing where your participants are coming from and how this may bias their view. Initially, focus more on whether they can complete a task or not, as opposed to whether they like the color you have used—and always be on the lookout for common themes or patterns across users.

Inviting People to Watch

In my experience, the minute people watch a user-testing session, they are sold on the value of it. No matter how much they might have argued against it initially, the value of this process is immediately apparent for all involved through watching a real person—from outside of the team or company—engage with an interactive model of your design. For this reason, I encourage as many people as possible from our client's world to observe these sessions (different business areas and team members), and I encourage you to also.

Your setup will ultimately determine who can come and watch. If you only have one room and no ability to record the session and have it play in another room for real-time viewing, you'll have to limit it to just one other person as you test with a user. Why? It is unnerving for the participant to sit in a room with many people watching every move they make. This can hinder the outcomes you receive, and is not ideal for the project.

Before you do any form of testing, consider who you'll invite and what type of setup is going to facilitate the best outcome for your users. Sometimes, it's useful to set guidelines for your observers. Encourage those watching to take notes and write down themes and issues as they perceive them; additionally, warn people to avoid jumping to conclusions off the back of one user.

This practice will assist when you discuss what design changes are needed at the end of each day of testing. It will help you to agree on and prioritize the updates that are to be made.

How do I set up a test environment?

By recording your research sessions, you're able to go back over session footage and extract new insights from the data.

A common misconception for user-testing is that you need a lab with a one-way mirror. In my experience, labs with one-way mirrors are unnerving for participants.

Even if no one is actually watching the sessions, your participant is being subtly reminded that their every move is being watched. It has a "Big Brother" effect.

Just like your up-front contextual research, you can go to your users' home or workplace and have them test your product on their own devices. There are many benefits in going to your users' environment: users feel less like they're being tested, and are often more relaxed because they're familiar with their own set-up and devices, despite the presence of cameras! Imagine how you'd cope in Figure 7.2.

Figure 7.2. Going into the wild

I've conducted testing sessions in some strange locations using some primitive re-cording equipment in the past; for example, I once ran a session at a user's house with my iPhone stuck to a wall with adhesive putty. It worked just fine! Nowadays, you have the ability to record anywhere, anytime, with a device that is likely to be in your pocket—making sessions conducted in the wild a whole lot easier.

In addition, there are all sorts of screen-capture technologies available on the market that show where the user clicks or touches, highlighting their pathway. Here are a few ways to set up a user-testing environment:

Create a portable lab setup

If you have a Mac, it comes with QuickTime Player built into OS X with a record function nowadays, allowing you to capture what is happening on the screen easily. ScreenFlow and Silverback are a useful combination to consider, as they record the user's face using the laptop's built-in iSight (or FaceTime) camera, and voice using the computer's microphone. You can also use screen-capture technology like Camtasia for later review.

Set up between rooms

In the past, office labs would have cables strewn between rooms, which was a logistical nightmare, not to mention a safety risk. Nowadays, it is possible to link rooms using WiFi between two computers connected to the same network. iChat (or Messages) has the ability to send screen interactions, and Skype can send the audio ... so cables be gone!

Test on mobile and tablet devices

You can mirror the screen of the iPad on a MacBook using screen-sharing software. You can then use Camtasia to record the session screen via the MacBook using Picture-in-Picture view. The beauty of this solution is that there's no clip-on camera trying to capture the screen, which gets in the user's way and is prone to screen glare or being knocked out of focus, as seen in Figure 7.3.

You can, of course, hire a lab if you want to be more formal. But even without a formal lab set-up, you can still conduct prototype testing.

Figure 7.3. Setting up testing in our lounge space

Choose the Type of Test

There are several reasons you conduct user-based testing at this stage, and the decision to do so will ultimately be driven by the product you're creating and what you want to achieve from the testing experience. Here are some of the types of testing on offer and situations you'd apply them in.

Usability Testing: How well does it work?

The basic reason for putting users in front of your product is to see if they understand the purpose of your design and do what's required.

For example, if you were creating an airline website, the most fundamental task to get right is the ability to buy a ticket. This task is the whole reason the site exists, so knowing that you've designed a simple and straightforward solution is critical to the overall success of the site.

To ensure the steps are dead easy, focus on when users can complete tasks to measure the overall efficiency of your design (that is, traditional usability). Watch to see if your users can complete the tasks you set with little or no prompting—and limited frustration. This should give you a good idea of how your design stacks up!

Concept Testing: Do users understand the concept?

Concept testing is worth considering when a new product is being developed. In these situations, the focus is not so much on the basic usability of the product; rather, you're interested in establishing whether users engage with and understand the wider concept.

This type of test is ideal for seeing how a future product or design might be developed, and is great when lots of new-to-market ideas are being explored. Concept tests can help you clarify the design problem or narrow your feature set.

In this test, the finer details of the interaction can be worked out later; the main focus is to gather initial reactions and impressions, and is less about detailed feedback on particular design elements.

Generally, you seek to prioritize your efforts for further design work, and learn as early as possible what concepts confuse, confound, or have low acceptance, or are worth developing or incubating a little more.

Design Evaluation: Which design is more engaging?

As you start to move through the various stages of wireframing and prototyping, you're likely to have started thinking about your product's visual design too. This often means that as you are playing around with the sequencing and task flows of your product, you're also designing a range of visually focused concepts.

User-testing is an opportunity for you to gain a reaction to a range of visual treatments. You should never overlook an opportunity to gain feedback from your users while you have them in the room.

You are looking for a reaction, or some emotional response from your users, rather than advice on layout or color. Emotional reactions are a necessary piece of the design puzzle, and can really help you determine whether a given approach is resonating with the audience, helping to guide the product design direction. Which design would you pick from Figure 7.4?

Figure 7.4. Testing different design concepts

Competitive Comparative Evaluation: How do users perform with comparable products?

Examining competing and complementary product offerings is an important part of the problem-solving process. This is no exception at the testing stage. Take a sample of your users completing basic tasks using some of these competing products to understand what works and what doesn't for your target segment. Try to understand why users react to different design patterns or features.

You perform testing as a comparison activity at the prototype stage by asking users to complete the same tasks across two or three offerings, with your prototype making up one of these. Sometimes it is useful to validate your own assumptions about what competitors are doing right or wrong. You might even find a client or a stakeholder is fixated on the way a competitor does something and wants you to design the final solution the same way.

Comparing competing products to your prototype helps to break down any preconceived assumptions around design patterns that should be followed, illuminating the right way forward. In this way, user-testing has been known to settle a few design arguments once and for all. Check out some competitor products we tested in Figure 7.5.

Figure 7.5. How do comparable products stand up?

Where the Action Is

Have you ever conducted user-based testing before? Have you observed user-based testing? Whether you watched a session or did one yourself, take a minute to think about what you learned, and how this would influence the way you'd perform testing in the future.

Session Script and Running the Session

A session should run as though it's a conversation with your user. It will put your user at ease and encourage them to open up about the design, making them feel less like they're undergoing an examination. You are definitely there to lead and keep conversation on track, so focus your discussion; however, following your script to the letter or being inflexible about improvising can lead to session outcomes of limited value.

Depending on the type of testing you're doing, your session script may vary. Nevertheless, it is important you create one so that you stick to a consistent approach across sessions and address important questions. Overall, consider it a guide—not gospel.

General Approach to Follow

The following points give a summary of how I structure my approach to running testing sessions:

1. Turn on the recorder and then fetch your participant. You should set up your camera and start recording *before* the participant is in the room so that you capture all the great comments made in the warm-up part of the session, not to mention remembering to record it.

2. Give a brief introduction that summarizes why the user is in the room with you and what you'll be doing at an overall level (this reinforces expectations and helps to clarify the structure of the next hour).

3. If you are filming, let them know this and ensure they're okay with it. Generally, recording is contingent on incentive payment, so most users are fine with this process—but it pays to check!

4. Request that users sign a non-disclosure agreement and sign off formally that they've received their incentive and are happy to be filmed. I give the incentive payment or gift to users up front, as I find it relaxes the user to have their money in their hand from the start, and prevents them from thinking I'll forget it later on, keeping them focused on the task.

5. Start with a review of the priming activity sent as homework with the recruitment specification. I find this activity helps to disarm the user and get them into the swing of talking freely and openly about the area of interest in an unrestricted sense. It captures online and offline behaviors and thoughts around the topic of interest (for example, "What does cooking mean to you personally?" was posed as homework to our users).

6. When finished discussing the priming activity, tell them that you'll be going through a number of tasks to which there is no right or wrong method; you are testing the design, not them. I also reassure them by saying, "If you can't do it, it's highly likely other people won't be able to either."

7. I quite often say I've had nothing to do with the design so that the user can criticize the design without feeling like they're offending me. Sometimes the participant holds back, because if you've been a good host, they like you and might wish to avoid offending you. So make sure you tell them it won't bother you either way!

8. Before you start reviewing tasks, take a breath and ask if they have any questions. Perhaps they'd like some water? Make sure they're comfortable and then dive into the testing part of the session.

9. Open with a broad question about the product, such as "When was the last time you used a site like this?", or "Do you use this site? If not, do you use ones like it?" Then encourage them to talk about why they use, or do not use, a particular product or service.

10. Remember the scenarios we discussed in the section called "Visualizing Task Flows and Scenarios" in Chapter 6 to determine the pages that needed to be prototyped? Use these to structure the tasks for your participant to evaluate the prototype. For each task, record if they completed it unprompted or not. If you are using a rating out of five, keep that clearly documented with your notes. I

tend to consider 1 or 2 a fail, 3 a pass, and 4 or 5 exceptional—this enables you to prioritize later when you analyze your results.

11. At the end of each session, ask these wrap-up questions: "What were your overall impressions? What were the top three things we need to do differently? How would you rate your experience out of 10 where 1 is woeful and 10 is wonderful?" Then set a post-test questionnaire, which we'll cover a little later in this chapter.

Don't be afraid to go with the flow and improvise. In time, you'll be better at deviating from a script and running the operation according to what makes the most sense, in order to get the most out of your user sessions.

 Scripting Tools

You'll find a user-testing host script including an example task list in the tools section of this book: **chapter07/user-testing-host-script.doc**. Download this template as a useful starting point for your own projects.

Running a Pilot Session to Fine-tune

We always make sure we run what we call a pilot session before testing, to make sure the session flows well and gives us the opportunity to iron out any wrinkles with the script.

A pilot session is a mock user-testing session, using anyone on hand (a team member, a colleague) to act as the participant. It allows you to run through the session script and decide if the wording of scenarios and the flow between tasks feels right.

Run a pilot session before you begin formal testing to minimize time wasted, and be on the lookout for the following issues:

Timing of the session	Set an hour and a half, maximum.
Flow, logic, and ordering of the scenarios	Be conscious of the order in which you ask users to explore different areas of your product.
The wording of scenarios	Read out loud the scenarios and check that they make sense to your mock participant, tweaking where needed.

Providing associated information	Offer sample information on a separate sheet of paper ahead of time, so that users have in advance what they need to complete tasks you have set.
Getting enough practice!	The pilot session is a chance for you to practice the routine at least once before you see a real user.

Watch How You Talk to the User!

The session should flow like a conversation, and you need to put the user at ease. It is important not to answer direct questions about what to do or how to do it.

Users can often feel unsure of themselves and, as a result, look to you for guidance on what to do. Try to turn the conversation around for them to give you a response. It's of no consequence how you think things should be done—the focus is on them. Consider the discussion in Example 7.1.

Example 7.1. Redirecting Users

User: Is that right if I click there?

Host: What are your thoughts?

User: I think I'd go there, but I wasn't sure about where to click ... is that right?

Host: What made you feel uncertain?

User: I guess I'd go there, oh right! Yes, that was it.

Host: Is there something that could make that action clearer?

User: I was unsure what [label] meant.

Host: What did it mean to you?

User: It wasn't the word I was thinking about ... don't you think cakes or desserts would be more useful?

Host: What is your take on it?

It's quite hard to avoid answering direct questions from your users. As you can see from the aforementioned discussion, there are many moments in which users will try to deflect to you instead of giving an answer themselves.

Close a Task if It's Going Nowhere

In contrast, it is sometimes necessary to intervene in order to complete a task. There's no point wasting time if a user is stuck or becoming frustrated and is unable to continue on to another screen that you need feedback on.

In these situations, I tend to score the task as a zero and say that we'll come back to it later; otherwise I'll lead the user to the page and ask for their feedback. You can use statements like "It seems you're having a bit of trouble completing that task, so how about we stop working on it and review it later?" or "If you're struggling, I'll show you the page where we'll find what we're looking for."

Remember, the longer you allow a user to flail around frustrated, the less likely you are to achieve what you require from the session. Users can rapidly lose confidence, and you might find it hard to get them back on track once they start feeling over-whelmed by it all.

Redirect Any Questions a User Asks

As a host, you really don't need to say too much; you're just required to listen and direct (or redirect). The statements I find most useful in these situations are:

- What are your thoughts?
- What is your preference?
- What is your take on it?
- How do you feel right now?
- Does it matter to you?
- What could help you in this instance?
- What do you suggest?

Anytime a question is posed directly to me, I use these statements to put the question back to the user. I've found that redirecting a question in this manner avoids making the user feel like they're silly for not knowing or being interrogated, or that you're evading a direct question. So remember to roll them out if you are stuck!

Roll Out the 5 Whys Again

I also find it useful to focus on "why" and "what" words in my responses, as they force the user to consider what they'd do and why they'd do it. Again, it helps you to extract an answer from them, instead of giving it away yourself.

Roll out The 5 Whys to help you run successful user-testing sessions that dig deeply around the reason users might think or act in a certain way.

Remember, your users might find it hard to articulate why they behave the way they do. The 5 Whys will assist you to probe into their actions and help to uncover contradictions between what they say and what they do.

Measuring Success of the Design

Establish up front how you'll determine success, and then follow a process for measuring it. That way, the entire team will be clear on why certain design updates are required or not.

One of the simplest measures is **task completion**; that is, could the person complete the task you set them? This basic measure will tell you what areas of the design require further attention and what sequence or workflows need improvement.

Here are some other metrics I've used in large projects, where many opinions are involved to help with collective decision-making:

- Assign an expert rating for task completion, where each task and the degree to which it is completed is ranked out of 5, giving greater perspective to issues than just a pass or fail (1 or 2 a fail, 3 a pass, and 4 or 5 exceptional).

- Ask the user for a subjective rating out of 10 (nominate the average you'd be satisfied achieving across all sessions, out of 10).

- Use the System Usability Scale (SUS) Score to give metric weight to outcomes. (The SUS score gives an ease-of-use score out of 100. As a group, you can nominate a number you'd be satisfied to achieve.)

There are other measures you could apply, but I find that using these few simple ones provides enough weight to decision-making. This is particularly so for those needing greater justification for design changes than user quotes alone provide.

Iterate the Solution

Once we have tested our prototype with end users, we can update our design approach based on the feedback we've received. The faster you use this information to update your designs and re-test it, the better. In UX, we refer to this as iterative testing and refinement.

Testing and refining an interactive prototype fast-tracks the traditional approach of market release, feedback, changes, and subsequent releases, but does so in a controlled environment where there's less to lose.

Remember our Angry Birds analogy? Iterative testing is just the same. Aim, fire, learn what you did wrong, and adjust. Then you repeat until it's ready for release. As Figure 7.6 shows, you should cycle through at least three iterations for confidence in your solution.

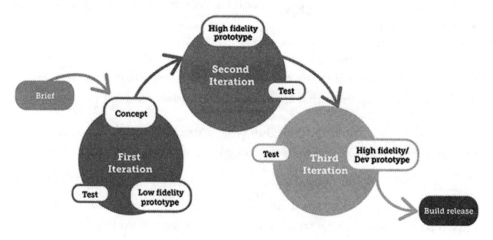

Figure 7.6. Test, learn, tweak. Iterate

This approach is effectively an incubator for immature designs. It enables the right environment for these designs to mature based on informed feedback from your users and subject matter experts, as well as constructive criticism from your client and your peers.

By focusing on iterative cycles of testing and design refinement, you gain more "bang for your buck" than two or three days of testing and one design update.

What does the process look like?

User-testing your design as it progresses allows for continuous feedback ahead of coding. Ideally, you should allow enough—but not too much—time to digest and communicate findings from testing with your team or client, so that you can jointly decide what to focus on in the next iteration.

As a broad outline, the following steps should be occurring across your iterative testing cycle:

1. Plan your testing sessions (this is the same as your initial testing plans).

2. Recruit the right users to ensure feedback is relevant (you should be a pro at this now).

3. Decide what to measure so you know how the design performed (this may vary over cycles, but you know what to do!).

4. Test up to four users a day for feedback (Done! We covered this earlier).

5. Review the outcomes and discuss the results with your team.

6. Update the design prototype based on these outcomes.

7. Test again with three or four users.

If you're doing several cycles of iterative testing, make sure changes sought from the client or your team are realistic within the time frame before the next cycle begins—there's a lot to do!

Making Sense of What You Observe

As when you were conducting contextual inquiries in the research phase, when you conduct user-testing sessions, you are looking for patterns across the sample that will tell you something about the design prototype.

Review Your Results Immediately

The process of analyzing your data formally is the same as described in Chapter 4. However, by the time you've reached this stage, you are usually more focused on feeding insights into the design or development team for changes to be made rapidly.

With a bit of luck, you'll have your client (or perhaps members of your team) watching the sessions, so take advantage of this and ensure you have daily outcomes you all agree to. Only create as much formal documentation as you need to communicate to a wider group, or those absent from the sessions.

At the end of each day of evaluation, I run a debrief session. I print out the design screens and put them up in the observation room for everyone to add comments while sessions are running. In a simple spreadsheet, I keep a log of the issues I have seen, and the team discusses whether they are a high, medium, or low priority. Finally, I create a high-level summary of decisions from day one of testing and distribute these.

There might be some gray areas that feel unresolved or unanswered. Embrace these for now and move quickly to the next iteration.

Variety Is the Spice of Life ... but Be Careful Interpreting!

You may see variability in the feedback among users who come to the sessions. Not all users are highly engaged, or able to discuss eloquently what they see or what it means for them personally. This is where you need to be part behaviorist/part designer.

When you find conflicting user feedback, you need to understand why the conflict exists. Ask yourself:

- Is it due to the different level of users' experience? (novice/expert)
- Have the scenarios been too specific?
- Did you lead too much in the way you asked questions?
- Were you over-sensitive in the way you reacted to the users' feedback?
- Are the goals of your testing session too vague?

Typically, you'll start seeing trends and patterns emerging across four users. If, however, your sessions leave you with more questions than answers, you need to review your approach and decide what went wrong. Whatever you do, avoid going headlong into design changes based on conflicting evidence.

Change for the Sake of Change

Beware of making wholesale changes based on one two participants' feedback. Only change what clearly needs it, and then monitor the impact at your next iteration of testing.

Once you've agreed on what needs addressing, you then must decide on a time frame for updates to be made to your prototype before you can test again.

Deciding When You're Done

The idea of a definition of "done" is used in the context of agile software development. It is worth noting that UX processes align very well with agile methods.

What is agile?

Agile is a group of software development methods based on iterative and incremental development.

There are many methods, but what distinguishes most agile processes are the development process, the mixed composition of teams, collaboration across disciplines, and adaptability throughout the life cycle of the project.

In agile processes, you break design and development tasks into small increments and focus on minimal planning and documentation, with agile cycles or **sprints** (a specified and consistent time period) containing requirements analysis, design, coding, and testing.

Behavior Driven Development (BDD) draws on agile methods and ensures scenarios are written before any code. These scenarios then drive the design effort, and, in turn, development process.

Many UX processes are now embedded successfully with agile development processes. Therefore, it is useful to consider how your UX process will contribute to agreeing when each cycle is done.

Having Clear Measures in Place

The iterative evaluation of your designs with users will give your client confidence in the current solution; however, sometimes there is disagreement over the quality of the outcome at a certain point in time.

Some measures and guidelines to assist in managing expectations include:

- agreeing up front to only two or three design iterations between days of testing (so if you are testing eight people, that is only two iterations; if you test with 12, that's three iterations)

- after the final iteration, everyone agreeing during the debrief sessions that 95% of the issues are resolved, and therefore everyone is happy to proceed

- checking that customer feedback is positive and metrics set earlier in your process meet the minimum standard that everyone agreed to (use the SUS score, expert rating of tasks, and subjective satisfaction scores)

- nominating to spend another sprint on design before moving onward if the client or a team member believes the design needs more work

These guidelines are merely intended as an example. You'll need to collaborate with your team and reach a consensus on the right measures for your situation.

Ultimately, agreement is influenced by budget, time frames, and the total scope of your work. Still, it is always a good idea to plan and have a clear structure, so that everyone is satisfied with the progress.

Case Study: Designing a Recipe App

In the section called "Visualizing Task Flows and Scenarios" in Chapter 6, we established that the first round of testing with our users would focus on the core functionality, and thus decided what the main user tasks would be. Next, we turned these tasks into scenarios that would make sense for a user to complete within the context of a user-testing session. The host script gives our conversations with users and the overall session some structure.

Setting Up the Lab

We have two labs at our offices: one for standard desktop evaluations, and a lounge room for tablet and smartphone device testing.

Basically, we mirror the screen of the iPad onto a MacBook using screen-sharing software. It would be ideal if the computer was able to receive the output of the iPad device in the same way a TV screen can, but this setup is unavailable at present, so that's why we need the extra software setup.

Once the iPad is mirrored on the MacBook, we treat this view as a website for usability testing, and use Camtasia to record the session using Picture-in-Picture format. The desktop recording captures the iPad screen, while the webcam captures the user interacting with the device and the conversation we conduct.

The user simply interacts with the device as they normally would, and we capture all we need without any additional imposition. This is important, as you want the experience to feel as real as possible for your participant, with no awkwardness in any aspect.

What We Focused on across Iterations

As a team, we agreed to have three or four iterative testing cycles of our prototype prior to launch. It allowed us to gather their impressions and view the design with fresh eyes.

This process gave us the confidence that when launched, the recipe app would work as intended and be simple, engaging, and fun to use.

The plan we followed for our iterative testing cycles was:

Round 1: Concept testing
   The initial prototype was a quickly pulled-together mix of images and hotspots. For our first iteration, we asked: How did users react to the concept? Did it make sense to them? Was it something they'd use?

Round 2: How well does it work?
   For round two, our more advanced design featured more mocked-up sample screens. We focused on making the prototype look more realistic (that is, having images of food we'd actually cooked ourselves rather than polished images, and

so on). All in all, we tested a more unified and resolved design in comparison to round one.

Round 3: Design tweaking

The next round was about tentatively exploring functionality slated for later releases, as well as perfecting the design and exploring more refined custom animations (for example, the movement between books, the navigation ribbon, opening and closing books, and flipping between friends' books and pages).

Round 4: Finalizing the design

The last round of testing was about fine-tuning and perfecting the microdetails of the recipe app's interaction design, and ensuring we had a few "wow" moments we were happy with, before starting to fine-tune the design to the high level of polish required to launch.

By the time we'd completed our iterative process, we had learned some critical factors we would not have obtained otherwise. We'll discuss some of the major learnings in the section called "Major Learnings".

Setting Measures in Place

As a team we agreed we'd plan for three or four iterations of testing, leaving it open for further rounds if we came to the final evaluation and felt that the design needed more work. Like most projects, however, it was our time frames that dictated if we would test more—and we were racing against the clock.

The measures of success we established for user-based testing sessions included:

- expert rating of task completion (1 to 5 scale)
- subjective satisfaction rating from users (score out of 10)
- System Usability Scale (SUS) (score out of 100)

The minimum scores from user-testing evaluation were set at: expert rating no less than 3 for all tasks; user subjective rating no less than 7 across all users; and a minimum SUS score of 70 across all users.

This set the minimum design standard we were after, with much higher outcomes expected by the fourth iteration (for example, expert ratings of 4 or 5; subjective ratings of 8 or 9; SUS score of 80 or 90). We were pushing hard with our expectations, but being a bunch of perfectionists, we could hardly settle for less.

We also wanted to observe in the user sessions a very high level of emotional engagement with the app. This is a somewhat subjective measure, but we wanted to gain a sense of this from what the user said and how they reacted or engaged with the concept. Was it an app they loved, hated, or were indifferent about? We wanted to see love.

Setting these measures in place up front allowed us to feel confident when it came time to finalizing the app and agreeing the design was ready to ship!

Major Learnings

Preparing for testing was generally hectic, as we finalized interactions and polished graphics. Some items we didn't manage to get working in the context of our main interactive prototype. These we loaded onto the iPad and showcased in static format, just to put the product in front of users for feedback, as shown in Figure 7.7.

Figure 7.7. Finalizing the prototype for testing

Following is a brief outline of some of the interesting "aha" moments we had from iterative testing with our users. There were many more than I've documented, but these ones impacted how we updated the design for the next iterative cycle. Some of the key insights included:

Round 1: Concept testing

Users reacted well to the idea of a digital recipe book, which was great! We learned that we needed to make content appear less like it had been styled for a magazine, and more as if a person had taken a picture at home and uploaded it to the book. Food needed to look like a friend had made it, rather than a publication's staffer. The choice of imagery really made a big difference.

Round 2: How well does it work?

For round two, we were interested in the basic usability of the design. We identified areas that were unclear to users, such as how to access friends' books from the home screen. As a result, we needed to reconsider the home screen layout. We then experimented with a "stack" of books the user could spread out on a virtual bench top, instead of the previous design that featured a line of books that the user had to scroll through.

Round 3: Design tweaking

The next round was about exploring functionality, as well as polishing the microdetails and our "wow" moments. More work was needed to anchor the experience within the book, and we needed to resolve issues around where people expected to see notifications and updates.

Round 4: Finalizing the design

For the last round of testing, we essentially had a fully working app that was how it would appear when downloaded and used for the first time. We focused on the first-time use scenario (invite friends, customize the book, create recipes, and so on), and gained valuable feedback on the team book and what sort of content would encourage users to come back to the app regularly. This helped direct our efforts around the marketing required to have the team book ready for launch.

Although this saw the end of our iterative user-testing cycles, we were yet to be done evaluating our product with potential end-users. In Chapter 8, I'll discuss what else we did pre-launch that enabled us to continue refining the recipe app design and functionality.

Build Up to Something

In this chapter, we've discussed the iterative testing and evaluation process that involves a working model of your product and a sample of your end-users.

The iterative cycle of testing, gathering feedback on your design work, and then updating and improving the design before you start the cycle again offers vital insights into the way users interact with and understand your design. Seeing the working model through your users' eyes allows you to understand what needs tweaking as you finalize your product for formal coding and launch. This enables you to learn ahead of the launch what makes sense to your users—at minimal cost. It can also help to uncover ideas or suggestions that you may have yet to consider.

In Chapter 8, we'll finalize our design and put the finishing touches on all aspects of it before we launch ...

Recap of What You Need to Know

Validating the UX:

- You are going to get it wrong the first time; testing interactive models of your work with users will guarantee better outcomes.

- You are too close to the design by now, so fresh eyes help to see matters differently. Have a plan for showing others what you have ready, and avoid being precious about your designs being 100% complete or all the issues resolved.

- Invite people to watch sessions so they see any problems encountered.

- No formal lab setup is required; you can go into the user's environment again, or set up a DIY lab with a camera and a few computers between rooms.

- Choose the type of test you are going to conduct:

  - usability testing

  - concept testing

  - design evaluation

  - competitive comparative evaluation

- Create a script and follow a session plan, but be sure to deviate from it or improvise where needed. Testing should be like a relaxed conversation rather than a clinical trial, but avoid answering direct questions: remember your 5 Whys.

- Capture some measures from sessions to reinforce the findings (for example, subjective ratings, expert ratings, SUS score, and so on).

Iterate the solution:

- Iterative means the act of repeating a process with the aim of achieving a desired end-result. Each repetition of the UX testing process is called an iteration, and the results are used to guide the next testing cycle or iteration.

- The number of cycles will be determined by the number of users you are involving (for example, two or three iterative cycles is standard), but agree to the parameters up front with your team.

- Review your results with your team immediately and gain agreement about what updates are required and in what time frames.

- Be cautious of making changes based on the strong opinions of one or two users, and always look for patterns and themes to emerge. The main issues or problems should be obvious to all involved.

Decide when you are done:

- Generally, time, budget, and scope dictate the parameters of when a project needs to be wrapped up; however, have some guidelines in place to assist the team in deciding when the design iterations are complete. For example:

  - the number of users to be evaluated and the design iterations in between

  - 95% of issues are resolved after all iterations are complete

  - customer metrics meets the level agreed up front with the team

  - if consensus cannot be reached, agree to one week of additional design updates, before moving onward

Where to next? Finalizing the design layer and readying to launch the product!

Launch to Learn About Behavior

At the start of our project, we began by trying to understand the design problem from the business's perspective. Then we went out into the world so that we could validate our thinking and gain empathy for the eventual users of our product.

Once armed with this knowledge, the UX process looked at sketching ideas and brainstorming with others as a way to explore design patterns and possible directions we could take. Following this, we created interactive prototypes of our design, in order to visualize a model of our thinking.

All the way along, we involved users as we tweaked, refined, and updated our design. As we face our launch date, our UX process has given us the best possible assurance that our product is going to work in the way we intend, once it's live.

In this chapter, we'll finalize the design and uncover user habits in order to change behavior in the future.

The Design Phase

The design (and development) stage of the UX process, shown in Figure 8.1, is all about the details of your product's design. It is a continuous cycle of design and development that will eventually see you finalize and launch your product.

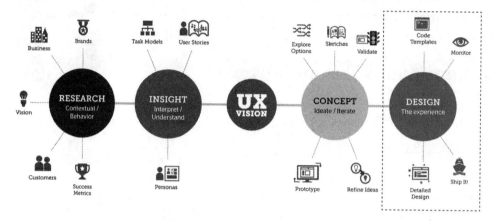

Figure 8.1. Design phase: The final stage in our process

This stage is usually the least glamorous, as we home in on every aspect of your product to ensure consistency, make final decisions on what is in and out, and then polish up the entire package so that we're ready to ship it.

The creative process associated with product design and development is hugely rewarding, but it can also be messy, stressful, and downright hard going. So well done—you are almost there!

 Launch Highlights

Take a minute to think about the products you have launched recently. What was your biggest focus in the lead-up to the launch? Where did you run out of time and where would you focus your efforts differently next time around?

Finalizing the Design

The final design is essentially the first release of your product. Everything that led up to this—such as following your UX process for exploration and iteration, and making the design simple and easy for your customers to grasp—has brought you to the point where you can now feel confident in the choices you're making.

As you reach this stage, resist assuming that your prototype will have answered every single design issue that your system or application presented during the implementation process. Quite often, there are still minor (and sometimes major) tweaks or adjustments to be made.

Armed with your solid understanding of your users, you can decide whether they can live with changes to the design at this stage of the process, or if it will cause undue confusion or dissatisfaction.

A Continuous Design Process

The design process is continuous, starting at the highest level with your design problem; then drilling into the details as you work from your prototype, turning it into a developed solution.

Despite the overall direction you've taken and validated with your users, the development process will inevitably raise issues that result in changes to your design as required.

This starts to look like an agile development process, whereby the design prototype gradually becomes the developed solution that is continually tweaked until the product is ready to launch.

You mean UX and agile are friends?

There is much debate around whether a UX philosophy and agile development are compatible, and quite often it will depend on the situation or circumstance in which you're working. In my experience, success depends on structuring the UX time frames around the agile environment in place. This is regardless of whether it is a small or large corporate environment that's implementing an agile approach.

Following a UX process gives clear goals and direction to the product you are creating, and delivering artifacts along the way reflects that big-picture strategy; for example, personas, competitor analysis, usage scenarios, interaction designs, sketches, wireframes, and prototypes.

To ensure the successful combination of agile and UX, start your UX process before your agile development begins. Figure 8.2 reveals the steps involved, beginning with research and insights, and then continuing with agile sprints merged with the concept and design stages.

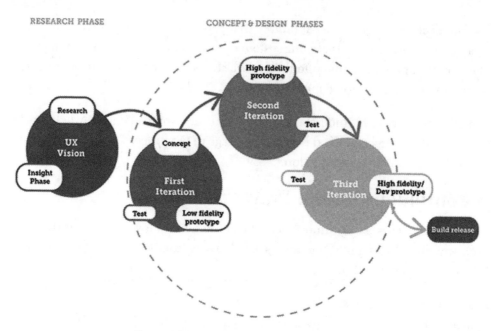

Figure 8.2. Merging UX process and agile development

Typically, the iterative and concept design cycles outlined in this book operate in a similar way to agile sprints. However, it's essential to make sure sufficient time is spent conceptualizing the complete experience and validating it with users before you start developing. Resist developing features in isolation from users, which is often the priority with agile development sprints.

You should also to remember to keep engaging with your users throughout agile development sprints. I've seen processes where teams fail to go back to their users to validate later iterations, but it is critical to do so.

As suggested in Chapter 7, ensure that everyone—developers included—agree to when you'll engage with your users up front so that it's scheduled, and not just an afterthought.

 Not-so-strange Bedfellows

What has been your experience with agile and UX? Did it work on your project(s)? What were your experiences and what would you do differently now?

Tweaking and Adjusting the Design

When you are forming your final design, keep in mind that you're still following a process of elimination and simplification. Perfection is a lot of little things done really well, so resist the temptation to "add value" where there's no need.

As you prepare to launch, your design and development efforts should aim to unify, simplify, and amplify. This means bringing all aspects of your design together, simplifying it as much as possible (without losing the intent), and then amplifying the design's key aspects that you expect will engage users.

This process illuminates the path for the user through your product, reinforcing the behavior you are hoping to see from them when they engage with it.

Beta Testing to Help You Tweak

It's really useful in the lead-up to launching your product to invite a small group of people to take part in a private beta test. **Beta testing** is a form of User Acceptance Testing (UAT) that releases a beta version of your product (basically a pilot version of the product) to a limited audience outside of the core project team.

 Test the Waters

User Acceptance Testing involves tests at the final stages of a project to ensure the product performs the minimum required business transactions. Often, a product must pass UAT before a client will consider the contract complete.

As with any final site edits, fresh eyes can help pick up things that might not be obvious to you. Beta groups engage with your product over a lengthy period of time to help you refine your design and technically test your product.

When selecting the beta group, choose experts from various fields to help you identify specific areas of improvement, so that you can harness their ideas across their domain specialties. We have found it particularly useful to focus on developers who perform bug testing and try out edge cases with the product.

Recruit some regular or target users along to see how general users might view your product. If you've been working on a rerelease of an existing product, seek users who have given well thought-out, constructive feedback in the past; perhaps even ask your more passionate users.

Invite twice as many people as you think you need. Chances are more than half the people you invite will disappear or find it hard to commit for the long haul, so make sure you have plenty of backup. If you can afford it, consider a cash incentive to keep their focus a little longer.

Chat to them regularly to keep them engaged, either online or in person; people are vocal at first, but sometimes they lose focus over an extended beta testing period. Expect more detailed design features and usability related feedback than longitudinal habit feedback during this process. (A longitudinal study involves observation of the same variables over an extended period.)

Use information gained from the beta group to help refine the first-time use scenario for your product. This group will help you perfect the initial experience that users will have with your product, so probe them on their first-time impression and gather ideas to improve it.

Seek feedback on the product's microdetails that stand out to this group. Did they notice the "wow" moments you planned? Were there aspects of your design they found annoying instead?

Make sure you use the feedback! There's no point gathering loads of good ideas if there's no time to address them, so establish a list of priorities and systematically work your way through it.

Beta testing helps you to fine-tune the design, correct any last-minute development and system issues, and gather feedback on a working model of your entire product, allowing you to tweak the details.

Help with Prioritizing Features

As you progress through detailed design, your backlog of desired features and functionality becomes your focus. Try to decide the optimal order to deliver different functional aspects of your design.

Beta testing can help you to identify features that are a hit and those that aren't without the emotion that might occur with team members or product owners. You may postpone some features to a later product release.

It's All in the Fine Print

UX documentation collates a range of best practices for interface design into a reference document. For digital products, it often includes the overall structure and how the user is expected to navigate through it. This supports an ongoing focus on ease of use by highlighting the usability standards expected.

Documentation for digital products also tends to cover more product-specific aspects, such as language or tone of voice, corporate style or branding, rules for presentation (color, logos, fonts, icons), and page or screen layouts (spacing, alignment, use of interface controls like drop-downs, buttons, and checkboxes).

Sometimes an archive of your sketches will help the team understand previous thinking that has informed the design. This saves them from going down old pathways that have been abandoned for good reason. Consider filing your original sketches in chronological order, or take photos of your sketches and put them onto a USB stick with all your associated project artifacts, so that they can be easily used as a reference.

Whatever you created through the concept stage to communicate to others the intent of your design is bound to be handy if handed over with the right instructions and format; for example, prototypes or interaction design documents. Don't be afraid to walk the team through it and see what they value most.

If you're not going to be part of the development process and are charged with creating documentation for another team, it's worth clarifying early in the project who the users of the documentation will be, so that you can tailor it to their needs.

When and how much should I document my designs?

Once the detailed design of your product has been finalized, it's time to document the design. When following an agile approach, however, documentation is often minimized or avoided. This is because the user research is incorporated into the development of the product.

Documentation that details the design can act as an educational tool, explaining the conceptual approach to the interface design, and helping to ensure that basic usability is built into the design from the beginning and continued with any future updates to the product.

The amount of documentation you produce will depend largely on your methods of working. For example, do you work alone or within a team? Do you design and develop your own solutions? Have you been engaged by a client as a third party? Your answers to these questions will influence the amount of documentation you'll need for an effective handover to another person, business unit, or company. Create as much documentation as required to convey the meaning and intended interactions of your design.

Generally speaking, those who will use your design documentation are specialists ranging from system architects, developers, business analysts, marketing specialists, or people working across quality assurance, depending on the stage of the project.

The artifacts I find most useful to include in UX documentation are:

- your prototype created as part of your design process: a living, breathing example of your design intent

- an interaction design document that captures each screen and details the design model

The Prototype as a Guiding Light

The prototypes you created as part of your iterative process are a roadmap for what is intended in the final build. Ideally, you would be present to help development teams work through design decisions in a collaborative manner, such as in an agile team—keeping the users and what would work best for them in everyone's minds.

If you're unable to be present, your prototypes are a useful reference point as they show the intent behind the interactive model of your design across key pages.

Make sure you update the prototype based on your last round of user-testing, so that the prototype represents the most current version of the validated design. Consider creating a "read me" file that details the key scenarios of use that drove its creation, as well as the areas that are clickable.

Interaction Guides

Interaction guides and prototypes, in combination, help guide developers and designers who make decisions in your absence as the build process continues.

Interaction guides are highly visual documents that describe the design in sufficient detail for another expert to understand and implement, as seen in Figure 8.3. They should have adequate annotations that allow a person to pick it up and gain a clear perspective on why aspects have been designed a certain way.

Figure 8.3. Interaction guides help describe the design to others

Here are some tips to creating effective interaction guides:

- Pay particular attention to document information such as the sequencing of steps, basic templates, links or controls, business rules or other constraints, and standard design elements (such as tables, callouts, and error messages).

- Reference any related documentation; this might include unresolved issues or general notes or comments.

- Construct a plan for maintaining the guide in your absence; this will better accommodate those people who might request changes or extensions to the document over time.

- Consider the format you choose to create. Why not put it online? Even consider a model that merges the working prototype and the interaction guide, showing design rules and guidelines in context.

■ Share it liberally! There is no point to creating documents if you don't share them with others. This builds shared understanding and support for your design direction, as well as awareness for the approach taken.

 How do you document?

What do you create as part of your final documentation and handover to the client or teams at the end of your projects? What has worked best in the past for you and why?

Final Checks and Balances

Checking your product before launch is like conducting a final edit; therefore, looking over all aspects in a methodical manner is crucial. In particular, consider consistency across your whole product.

There are a bunch of checklist-style resources on the Web that can help, so rather than go into exhaustive detail, I'll highlight some key points to get you started.[1]

Visual design elements

Images and assets need to be highly polished. Ensure you check consistency across the whole product, and do final checks against brand and the overall marketing message.

Content

Read over every page and check for consistency. Make sure there are no spelling errors, that headings are sufficiently descriptive, and that any test content has been removed.

Navigation and information structure

Check that links are consistent and easy to identify, and that there is a logical sequencing and task flow throughout your product. Verify that labeling and grouping of information assists your users in locating the core content of the site.

---

[1] Have a look at *Smashing Magazine*'s list of 45 questionnaires and checklists for pre-launch of online products, a great starting point for creating your own lists:
http://www.smashingmagazine.com/2009/06/29/45

Technical testing

Perform final technical tests (system, integration, regression, and load tests, for example) and User Acceptance Testing of your product before launch to guarantee that there are no nasty surprises once you go live.

Coding standards and accessibility

Confirm that you are meeting requirements in terms of standards expected or set for your product (by your client and also by the industry).

Marketing and promotion

Consider what is scheduled for the lead-up to launch, what will happen once you go live, and what occurs in the weeks following. Make sure you are working with and talking regularly to those who own this task—you only get one chance to make a splash.

What is in and out

Evaluate the features or aspects of your design that are yet to be resolved. Keep a list of what remains and update it daily; if the list is distributed, ensure you're across who's doing what.

 Launch list? Check

If you've yet to do so, I'd encourage you to create your own product launch checklist that you can follow for each project. Construct a list around what has worked best for you in the past and update it after each project, based on some of your own timely learnings.

There are several goals that your product should be achieving right now, so it's a great time to validate this one last time before you launch. Following a UX process from end to end will reassure you that your product is going to be well-received by users, but testing before launch can be useful in picking up issues that were undetected until the whole product was pulled together as a fully functioning unit. It's also a great way to double-check that any details done at the last minute still make sense to users and haven't compromised the overall product intent.

How are you feeling about your product?

When it comes to the final weeks or days before you launch your product, one of the biggest indicators of readiness is how happy you are feeling. Your happiness radar is a bit of a subjective, gray area, but the measures you've taken along the way should give you confidence that your design is ready for launch.

Here are a few questions to ask yourself:

- Are you happy with the design?

- Have you unified, simplified, and amplified the product's core content and features?

- Is the product as simple as it could be?

- Are the "wow" moments as you expect—do they stand out sufficiently?

- Does it represent a significant improvement on what was there before (if there was a predecessor)?

- Have you done enough to ensure the product will stand apart in a crowded marketplace of like products?

- How do you feel when you revisit the product after a break from it for a few days?

 Happy Days

Reflect on what you look out for with your design work to indicate that you are finished and ready to launch. What are the signs that let you know you are happy with your design?

Uncover Habits to Change Behavior

Design changes behavior: fact. Throughout this book, I have emphasized that understanding behavior is vital to ensuring that you can nudge users towards doing what you want them to do with your product; but, if you fail to understand your users' habits, how can you hope to change their behavior?

Habits, of course, are not black and white. They tend to be strong or weak. The more automatically you perform a behavior, the stronger the habit is.

Remember, you need to consider your users' habits before you design, while you design, and after you launch your product if you're going to understand how to impact users' behavior with your product.

In Chapter 2, I encouraged you to explore and uncover users' behaviors and your client's behavioral goals. Then review your original behavioral goals.

Learning about Behavior

Everything you've been doing up to this point has been about getting your product out there to see if it resonates with the users for whom it's intended.

There are a lot of buzzwords floating around that are essentially just a new way to explain why we follow certain aspects of the UX process (think Lean, Lean UX, Agile, Guerilla, MVP, and so on).[2]

I'll avoid explaining these ideas, as I believe the terms used to describe what we are doing will always shift as new ones emerge. What's important is that we're learning about our prospective customers' behavior as we develop our product, and using this information and insight to shape our design approach. This ultimately helps us to decide what features will matter most.

Pre-launch Assumptions

So what should be learned once your product launches?

There are several factors to consider before you launch your product, and then to be on the lookout for once you've launched so that you can monitor how successful it will be long-term. These include:

Intrinsic value	Try to quickly ascertain what users appear to value about your product.
Possible hurdles	What is limiting uptake or use of different aspects of your product?
Survival of the fittest	Are you managing to hold your own against competitors, and offer value beyond them long

---

[2] See the popular book by Eric Ries, *The Lean Start-up*, for a detailed view of this approach to building software (New York: Crown Publishing, 2011).

enough to differentiate your product and thwart attempts at being copied?

Habitual users   What will make customers fall in love with your product, or even become addicted habitual users of it? Are they using it over and over again, inviting and encouraging others to do the same?

Scalability and growth   Are there enough people out there who will find value in your product, so that the audience pool will grow over time?

Viability of your product   Can you leverage the growth of your product's popularity enough to turn it into a viable and sustainable revenue stream?

How will you interpret all this data? You can do so with an unwavering focus on your users' behavior once your product has launched, and a series of measures that will allow you to shift the dials on your design when it is out there in the marketplace. Then you can nudge users' behavior in the desired direction, based on a clear understanding of the habits emerging around your product's usage. Does reading an infographic such as that in Figure 8.4 help you understand user behavior?

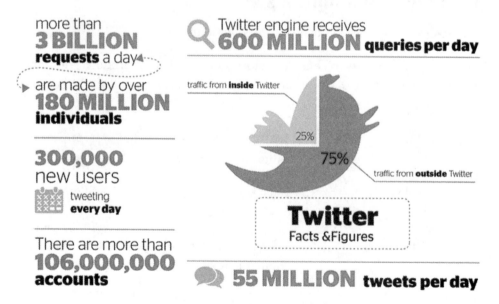

Figure 8.4. Measuring behavior before and after release

Gaining a rapid understanding for how your product is being received will help to shape your overall product strategy and impact the future release of features and functions.

What makes a habit?

When you think about some of the great technology solutions of the last 20 years, many share a common ground: they create a habit. When technology has created a habit in people, a person's use of a product is automatic, without thought.

Technologies with a social aspect are clear winners in the habit-formation stakes. Facebook, Pinterest, and Twitter all have users coming back to their sites several times a day to check what has been said, posted, or liked about content—sometimes even several times within an hour.

The additional game-changer in habit formation has been the explosion of mobile devices. Even traditionally non-habit forming sites that are more transactional in nature have the ability to become habit-forming when made available on a mobile phone (for example, mobile banking). Consider how smartphones have changed how we interact with business, as shown in Figure 8.5.

Figure 8.5. Smartphones: changing the way we do business

Products used daily create a barrier to entry for competitors in their market. If your users are unable to imagine life without your product, you can safely say you've met your goal. So what makes a habit?

The more you do something without making a conscious decision, the stronger the habit. Frequency of use leads to the creation of a habit in your users; so if your users are coming back regularly, it's likely that habits are forming. Consider Figure 8.6.

Figure 8.6. Can you imagine life without your cell phone?

 By Force of Habit

Before we discuss how to measure your users' habits once you've launched, how do you think you'd tackle this? Have you ever considered this before? If yes, what have you done in the past? What has worked and what hasn't?

How do you measure a habit?

Measuring the effectiveness of your design in creating habits can be broken down into those tasks you perform before you launch, and those that you do after.

Before You Launch Your Product

Define a habitual user

How often do they use the site? What do they do? How long do they stay? How often do they visit? These questions will help you to outline what you are expecting up front before you launch. This is easier to do if your product already exists, but try to estimate what you'd expect or hope for, at a minimum.

Define the frequency of use

How many times a day, week, or month do you see as realistic usage? Set a clear expectation for overall frequency of use of your product, but try to be realistic. Everyone wants users to engage daily, or even hourly—but few products manage this. The context of your product will help guide what you can sensibly expect.

Use the product yourself

Keep note of how often you use your own product. Average out your ideal-use scenario with the number of times you have used it; adjust expectations from there.

Focus on behavior

Remember, we are focused on users' behavior, and what creates a habit varies for the type of service you deliver. Focus on individual users and what they are doing, and assess if they're making your product a habit or not. The overall active user rate is not predictive; it is what they are actually doing that should be the focal point.

After You Launch Your Product

Set the baseline

Once launched, you are in a position to collect and analyze data around habits. Measure at intervals how many of your users actually fit the definitions you set at baseline, and then at different time periods post-launch (monthly, quarterly, six-monthly).

Who is dropping off and why

Understand who engages with your product and who dumps it. Try to uncover why that might be the case using UX methods.

Crunch your numbers

Watch as user data and patterns emerge and then see how many of your users actually meet the expectations you originally set. If no one is using the product in the way you expected, then decide from your audience pool what they are doing and monitor as behavior changes or adjusts over time (a few examples of monitoring tools to consider include Flurry, Localytics, Google Analytics, ClickTales, and so on).

Be patient!

Measuring behavior is a job done longitudinally and there is no way of hastening time. The best results are taken over a long period, and during this time anything could change—so hang in there. There are also slow starts.

There is no magic percentage you can assign to assess whether your product is creating a habit. Actual user behavior patterns are most predictive of an eventual habit.

Monitor your users' movements through the product, engage with them (for example, through interviews and evaluations), and continue to watch and learn.

Evolution, Not Revolution

Iteration as an approach to learning continues even after you've launched, and is backed (or refuted) by larger volumes of customer data that reflect actual use of your product.

You need to take these learnings and continue to evolve your design, but keep in mind that it is about evolution rather than revolution at this stage of the game. You are not looking to fundamentally change your design approach, but rather to tweak and refine based on a new level of understanding of your customers' needs and habits, as shown in Figure 8.7.

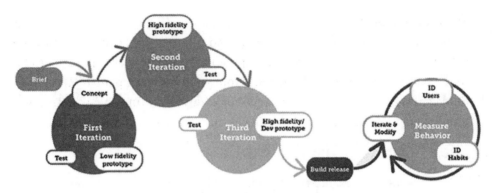

Figure 8.7. Continual learning and iteration

Observe the Early Adopters of Your Product

Watching the early adoption of your product will allow you to ascertain where the real value of your product lies for your users, helping you to then shape the product in new or unexpected ways.

A great TED talk with Evan Williams, the co-founder of Twitter, reveals how watching early adopters of the product helped to uncover hidden value that was not imagined in its creation.[3]

In this talk, Evan discusses how Twitter was originally created as a broadcast medium. Users shaped its evolution by inventing ways of doing things; for example, using the @ handle evolved from users shouting out to other users they knew whom they wanted to draw into their discussions; it was not part of the original design.

Similarly, the use of the hashtag [#] to search for like items was not originally designed, but created by a third-party provider as a way to locate content as the service grew and evolved. Twitter then purchased this service, and the hashtag became an invaluable way of locating content across all posts.

What does a habitual user look like?

Once you've launched, identify the behaviors that differentiate your habitual users from the rest, and try to identify the tipping point that took them from normal user status to habitual user status. It will take more than stats to uncover the answer,

---

[3] http://www.ted.com/talks/view/lang/en//id/473

and this is where follow-up contact with your users will be useful to uncovering the "why."

Before you go see users in the wild, check your data and formulate a hypothesis about their usage and why they might have taken a certain pathway that other users have not.

Model Your Top Users' Habits

Target your devoted users and try to understand their usage and behavior in detail so that you can apply learnings from this group to the rest of your user group. Understand what it was that hooked them more strongly than standard users so that you can then use this information to attract a new group or convert others.

You could focus on data and drill down to see what they did and where they went within your product, uncovering the patterns and areas that drove their usage. Alternatively, pull out your UX methods again and talk to your most passionate users about how they use the product; monitor them in their own context and ask them to keep a diary through the trial so that you can uncover greater detail than stats alone can give you. Your devotees will love it!

Identify from your data commonalities among the habitual users to see if there is a pattern that led to a habit that can be translated across a wider group.

UX Is Critical to Habit Measurement

Usage statistics are invaluable as a first step as they give you a high-level idea of how people are using your product; however, users can be interrupted in different ways, and what you see in the data might not be the result of the design. Instead, it may reflect a certain situation or circumstance. Like everything, data needs intelligent interpretation.

In many ways, we come full circle in our UX process. To uncover habitual behavior, use benchmark testing, contextual interviews, and diary studies. In your diary studies, you can leave a select group of users with your product and monitor usage over an extended period of time—say, two weeks to two months—and ask them to record instances of use and general notes about the product.

UX helps you to see what is most valuable and habit-forming about your product, so that you can create something that really resonates and makes a difference to your users and the wider product landscape.

Modify Based on What You Learn

What you learn post-launch will allow you to focus on aspects to further develop and refine your product. You'll also be able to market your product to new users in a way that directs them towards the end you seek. What end were they aiming for in Figure 8.8?

Figure 8.8. Reinforce the behavior you want to see with design

To reach a deeper level of understanding, head out of the office and start talking to the real users of your product once again. This should help you to add context to the analytical data you've collected. Key areas for expanding your learning at this stage are:

- What are hurdles to engagement with the product or features, if any?

- What gaps do competitor's products fill that yours don't?

- Is the problem your product solves one that customers want solved?

- Are your strategies influencing users' behavior towards the desired result?

■ Which aspects of the product resonate with users, and which do not? (In this sense, you understand the aspects of the original vision that have been validated, and those areas that are not resonating.)

Remember: with product design, it's about evolution, not revolution.

Case Study: Cook the Recipe App

Now we've reached the last part of our UX journey, let's look at our case study of developing a recipe app.

The Name Game

The initial idea behind the app was to preserve family history and heritage by creating a digital version of a treasured family recipe scrapbook. This drove the name—Family Favorites, as seen in this wireframe in Figure 8.9—and it stuck for a long time.

Our contextual research and user interactions from our UX process highlighted two key segments. They were:

Foodies   unmarried, or married with no kids; focus heavily on sharing, preparing, and generally loving all things gastronomic! Happy to spend lots of money on ingredients, and would love nothing better than cooking for dinner parties with friends all weekend

Family caterers   married with kids; used to live the foodie life, but with the focus now on family, their love of food is on hold while they manage a hectic life and juggle several demands; quick and easy is the order of the day

Research in our concept and design phases revealed that Foodies felt that the name of the app excluded them. Therefore, we had to reconsider the name so that it would appeal to a broader audience.

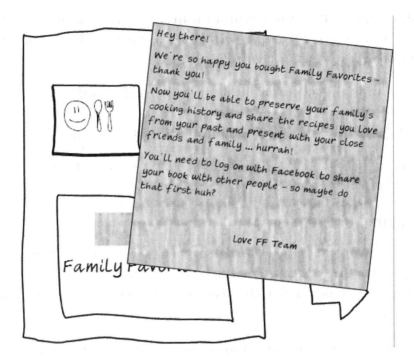

Figure 8.9. Personality, but missing the mark

We wanted to have a name that represented what the app offered users. The main purpose of the app was to facilitate creation and storage of treasured recipes, while enabling you to swap them with your friends.

As a result, we narrowed our focus to two options: Cook and RecipeSwap. What tipped us over to Cook was that we were yet to establish if the swapping capability of the app would be the main drawcard. We'd only find this out once the app was being used in the wild, so the name might limit the app long term.

We also wanted the name to reflect the essence of creating recipes, sharing them, and using them. Cook is more all-encompassing, as it's all about cooking. So Cook it is.

Naming Conventions

Have you ever named a product before? What was the process you went through? How did you decide on the final option?

Where did we start out and then end up?

At the beginning of the recipe app project, we set ourselves the goal of finalizing the product within six weeks.

Once we kicked off and reached the research and concept stages of our process, however, we further considered—like many before us—what we were creating, and the features and functions we'd need to deliver.

Rather than focus on this arbitrary time frame, we directed our attention towards getting the details of the app right. We explored the interactions of core features we believed were needed at a minimum. We gained a new appreciation of just how challenging it was going to be to implement, and, therefore, how long it would realistically take to finalize the product.

Our original time frames gradually increased from what we thought would be a rapid startup—six weeks—to a lengthier product development cycle of 20 weeks.

Review of the Design Process

Apart from its ability to create and manage your favorite recipes, the main feature of the app was going to be its social aspect. Cook would allow the user to invite friends to access their book, so they could view recipes, add them to their own books, and, most importantly, be able to comment on each other's recipes.

Adding social capability was probably the biggest design challenge we had to deal with in our concept and design phases. Handling notifications and comments elegantly was a harder task than it initially appeared, mainly because the app's premise was focused around books; there was no real central area that a newsfeed of comments or updates could logically sit. Figure 8.10 shows the limits of positioning news content in our existing designs.

Figure 8.10. Laying out the grid for Cook

We tried placing comments on the bench top, and then investigated a newsfeed of sorts within an "activity" book. Eventually we settled for updates listed at the front of each person's book (the first few pages) before they move to the recipes. When the user came to their book, there would be a clear indication of what activity had taken place before they even entered, as the design in Figure 8.11 shows.

Figure 8.11. Handling notifications and social elements

In order to have a cluster of notification alerts as one entered the app, we moved from a line of books on a bench top to a stack of books in a pile. This stack could be spread across the user's bench top once they entered, and elegantly consolidated what activity had been occurring since they last visited.

Once spread out, the user could move between their friends' books to see what was new in each. The books could be toggled to show those that had updates, or the user could scan their book list in an A-Z format. Books with new content would be marked by photos sticking out, as Figure 8.12 shows.

Whenever we had a tough design problem to solve, we had to remind ourselves it was all about "the user's book" and revert to whatever solution we felt best preserved that metaphor.

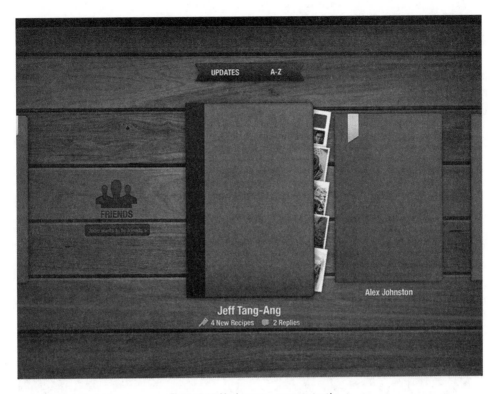

Figure 8.12. You've got ... new content!

One of the microdetails we were stuck on when it came to development was movement between the user's book and their friends' books. We wanted this gestural movement to be a significant interaction.

There was to be a distinct feeling of resistance as the user moved from their main book to another book on their bench top; concurrently, we wanted the bench top to shift ever-so-slightly in the opposite direction as they moved across it, creating a visual illusion of movement and resistance. Could this be a "wow" moment? We thought so.

Custom code was required, and our developer took some weeks to refine this approach—but he nailed it. Happy days!

As the detailed design progressed, we reconsidered how to manage "friends." Instead of just going to an overlay or a separate settings area as many apps do, we decided to opt for an address book on the bench top that could prompt the user to follow new users—or even invite new users. This design meant we could potentially put a spotlight on a celebrity chef or restaurant/café to allow users to "follow" them, reinforcing a behavior we wanted to see in our users.

From a behavior design perspective, this also meant the book had activity that would draw users back more often, as featured chefs would upload recipes more regularly than friends might; after all, we needed a reason to bring users back to help create a habit. Figure 8.13 reveals our address book on the bench top.

Figure 8.13. An address book of friends and chefs to follow

We felt we'd designed a great way to keep the idea of following and inviting new users top-of-mind; instead of hiding the contact area, we exposed it—design win! In an offhand way, we mentioned to our developer that we wanted the user to have the same resistance between moving from their list of current friends' books to their address book.

Um … problem.

Our developer spent three weeks trying to create the custom code for this before suggesting we try a few design alternatives that might be easier to code.

This wasn't the only problem that forced us to review the way we finalized our design, but it does exemplify the continuous design and development cycle that is typical of this last stage in the UX process.

UX and Agile ... Yup! It Works

As we mentioned earlier in the chapter, there's a lot of contention around whether an agile development and UX philosophy can work together in harmony; this project has followed both approaches and has managed to combine them successfully.

There are a few points that need to be considered to allow a successful outcome, which are:

The make-up of the team
> We have had designers, developers, and UX designers and researchers all in the same room collaborating for the entire process. This has been essential, as different skills were brought to bear on problem-solving.

Research and insight head-start
> Contextual research kicked off our process and insights were fed into the design concept stage. The concept stage saw us creating prototypes, where we jumped from wireframes with clickable or hotspot interactions straight to developed code (starting hacky and then refining as we progressed). Design and development exploration occurred in parallel for us, and this worked well, as custom animations often meant cycling back into what could and couldn't be done in a design sense.

Parallel research
> We scheduled much of our UX research and user engagement to happen in parallel to the design and development sprints that were occurring; this meant that user feedback was collected iteratively and continually fed into the design and development effort.

Our research meant that useful conversations about features and prioritization of these could occur up front and then throughout the remainder of the development process, helping us avoid a backlog.

As our concept design prototype evolved into the developed solution, decisions were impacted by the practicalities of whether or not what we initially imagined was technically feasible. The two happening in tandem meant we changed approach when necessary, and didn't waste too much time.

Overall, the two worlds can fit well; however, I do feel it depends on the make-up of your team. Our team was predominantly UX designers and researchers, meaning that forgetting our users as we moved through design sprints was unlikely.

Focusing on "Wow" Moments

Our app would be used in the kitchen while someone is cooking, and our research and consequent analysis process presented some development features that would help make the app more useful to users, while also making it unique in a development sense. Two points struck us when researching:

- Those who used a device had to keep unlocking the screen to read the ingredients (not realizing there is a setting they can use to prevent this).

- Those who used a device when cooking were concerned about dirtying their device with food-covered hands (for instance, struggling to move through pages while trying to use a clean part of their knuckle).

We wanted to ensure our design overcame both these situations, so a technical and development research process ensued. The first issue of unwanted screen-locking was easy to resolve.

The other situation called for an investigation of gestures, so that a user could swipe a hand or move their arm for an interactive gesture without having to touch their device.

Both of these weren't really design-related at all; however, the benefit of our collaborative group was that our developers could research how the gestures might be possible as we continued with detailed design for other areas of our app.

We felt that the gestural page-turn or actions to scroll through ingredients would be one of those microdetail "wow" moments when using Cook.

Beta Testing the App

After our iterative user-based testing cycles were complete, we put in place a list of people we would invite to our beta test group, so that we could gain detailed feedback on the app over a longer period of time.

We basically took two approaches to this step that I'll detail for you now:

- One group was our expert group of users (developers, designers, and a range of peers and friends). These users lived with the design for a month, so that they could give us feedback and help us identify elements that needed more attention. The developers who assisted in this process were doing some general function and bug testing, as well as testing out some edge-cases.

- The other group was our research user group (two users from our research and iterative testing process). We gave these users iPads with the app for the same month of beta testing. This enabled us to see what some average end-users loved or hated about the app, and helped us prioritize changes and make last-minute tweaks to the design.

What was the process and benefits?

Using two test groups worked extremely well and I'd suggest you try it out. The process we followed included:

- The beta testers from both groups were very keen and passionate at first. We set up distinct Yammer groups, and this enabled live chat and discussion one-on-one or among group members. The discussion from the two groups had such a different focus that we felt they should be kept separate.

- As noted earlier in the chapter, the attention and focus of the expert group lowered across time, but not for the user group—we paid them a cash incentive for their time. This helped us to keep the users engaged, and meant that they took the task more seriously across the extended time frame.

- At a minimum, one of the team would post a key question to each group once a week. There was also some form of daily contact, with one of us confirming something with either of the test groups that was usually tied into the design and coding.

- We planned two behavioral interview sessions with our users, one every two weeks of the beta test process. This allowed us to have a face-to-face discussion with the users about their experience and what they thought generally.

- These sessions were very much like an exploratory user-testing session. They allowed us to watch the user with the app, and gain a sense of why they might have thought or felt a certain way, as well as observe how they used different design features and elements. This gave us great ideas for what to change and update based on what we were seeing and hearing.

The interview process is a little like a diary study—but using the real app. Insights helped to refine and tweak the app and elevate the design; this progressed it even further than when we left off from our formal iterative user-testing process.

Expert Research Group: the Team!

From the moment we had our first working prototype, team members loaded it onto their own iPads and were living and breathing the app.

Each new development update was sent from our developer to the wider team, keeping everyone across the refinements as they occurred and the overall approach being taken.

This allowed us to home in on the sequencing of different steps, and design features that we needed to improve and refine. In turn, we were able to evaluate what would give the app several "wow" moments, which ones actually were "wow" moments, and which ones still required work. It also helped us to imagine the areas that might be habit-forming, ahead of the official release.

What documentation was useful?

The design and prototype of the app formed its documentation. Given the size of the team working on the app, there was no need for formal documentation. We did, however, start an experience guide, so that we had a clear reference to the style, interaction, and other design aspects for all designers to share as they came on and off the project.

Once we moved past a certain stage of prototyping, the prototype itself became a working model, which meant coding was being finalized in parallel.

Because our team was small and spoke daily, there was little need to communicate the overall intent to people who came along later in the process or would generally be absent.

Approval for Our App to Launch

The final hurdle for the recipe app was to submit it to Apple post-development and wait for approval. Nowadays, this process generally takes between seven to ten days, but can take longer.

For the last few months, we have met with Apple representatives to gain their feedback and advice on the design as we tweaked and perfected it; this meant they were now familiar with the app and where we were taking the overall concept.

Once approved by Apple, the app can be automatically released, or held waiting for us to nominate a release date. Our goal is to craft something special so that we're featured in the App store. Given the exposure this provides, it's a healthy start for our modest app.

Our Total Experience Vision for the App

Right from the start of our process, we've tried to imagine a broader experience for our app users than just an iPad app.

We believed that for the app to be compelling and create habits in our users, we'd need to ensure the following: simple, social, and encouraging habits. We had simple and social covered, but encouraging habits was harder. What would encourage a user to immediately think to upload a recipe to our app and spend the time doing this, against their current ways?

It was about having a digital store of someone's most special recipes, preserved for life. The ability to take a picture of an original recipe and upload it, or create a summary quickly, was going to be critical. However, we felt it was the link to the offline world that would really drive and encourage use.

We wanted to make sure one of the app's features was to enable ordering and purchasing of the book as a hard copy, so that users could send it to family and friends, or just have for themselves.

People love the tangible nature of books, and there is something nice about the tactile feeling of flicking through a book for inspiration. We needed to wait and see how users engaged with the product once launched, and planned a teaser for what they could do once they had enough recipes stocked up to help encourage the creative aspect of the app.

Researching Books for Printing

Currently, we are researching print options and different styles of books and designs. This would mean that, once ordered, the book would take on a similar but slightly different appearance to the book layout and design within the app. We wanted to ensure there was an additional "wow" moment when the user received their book in the post, and a distinct look was one way to achieve this.

We also wanted to deliver a "wow" moment with the unboxing of the book, so researching the packaging with the idea of delivering a different kitchen implement with each book (such as a spoon, a tea towel, a whisk) is also underway.

These items will be delivered in a future release of the app, once users have been able to accumulate recipe information and we've had the chance to monitor how many recipes books they tend to use on average.

These are the microdetails that will make the overall experience with our app more emotional, and therefore more memorable.

Our Focus on Behavior Design

Throughout this book, I hope to have impressed upon you that design has the ability to change people's behavior. This is probably a new way for you to think about your design work—but a critical shift to make.

Understanding what would need to change about a user's current habits for them to adopt our product was an essential way to think about the design problem that lay ahead of us. So how did we try to address these behavior ideals in the design of our app?

Deconstructing the Behavior Design of the Recipe App

The app itself was a digital cooking scrapbook. If people downloaded the app, it could be assumed they'd use it for this purpose.

This supports one of our original behavior goals:

- Users will create and store recipes within a digital space.

Ensuring that the app had a social component would encourage users to share and invite friends and family to the app.

The address book was specifically designed to sit on the bench top and always be present at the end of the user's book list. That way, they were prompted to invite new friends or follow chefs or restaurants we might have spotlighted and placed into this area.

We also created a "featured" book as a tool to help us capture the user's attention and bring them back to the app, even if they had no need to upload a new recipe.

This helps supports our other goals:

- Users will share recipes with others via this space.

- Users will invite family and friends to this space.

- Users will check the app regularly and engage in dialogue with others.

One of the concerns from research was that users didn't put many recipes into their special cooking scrapbooks, and this was for a number of reasons. First, they had limited space (digital overcame that for us and would encourage use, we hoped); second, they were picky about what recipes went into these books.

To address this last aspect, adding a recipe needed to be simple and enjoyable, and we had to ensure there was intrinsic value in people having a digital copy of their recipes for sharing with others.

This supports these behavior goals:

- Users will abandon paper and pen formats.

- Users will document day-to-day meals and not just "special occasion" food.

- Users will feel compelled to document all their culinary experiences in this space.

The ease and simplicity of documenting culinary experiences in Cook is shown in Figure 8.14.

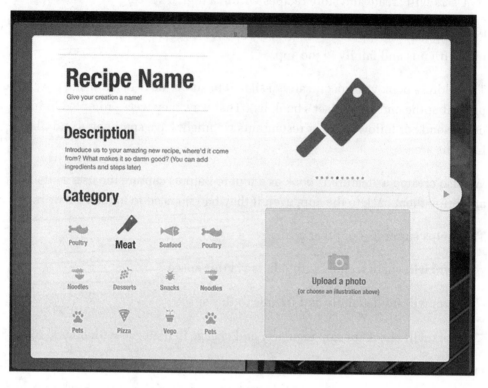

Figure 8.14. Simplicity is the secret sauce

Some of these behaviors would need to be watched after the app was released and reviewed in post-launch in-context interview sessions; for now, we felt we had addressed ways to ensure the app encouraged habits to be formed in our users.

Post-launch habit and behavior tracking is a longitudinal job, one that we'll keep reviewing with a combination of data analysis and quarterly user research that will take us into the homes of our users. This will allow us to continually update and tweak the design of the app, based on what we learn.

As always, your continuous design process is ongoing, but it is focused on evolution as you learn, not revolutionary changes to your design. For now, our app looks like Figure 8.15.

Figure 8.15. Let's Cook

Concluding Thoughts

Sometimes, when we sit down to design and explore the interactions we need, the user is lost from our thoughts as we focus heavily on the object we're designing. This can lead us to lose sight of the bigger picture.

A great quote by Mark Weiser reminds us what matters most when it comes to our design work:

> "The most profound technologies are those that disappear. They weave themselves into the fabric of everyday life until they are indistinguishable from it."[4]

—Mark Weiser

---

[4] Mark Weiser, "The Computer of the 21st Century," *Scientific American* Ubicomp Paper, 1991, pp 66-75.

Keep remembering that your design will influence and shape the way people live their lives. Think about your users, the types of behavior you want to evoke through your design, and the future interactions you want to enable with your product when you design, as often as you can.

What will help remind you to do this?

Understand your business problem and embrace the constraints that you may have thrust upon you. Solve your design problems by embracing the user's viewpoint; sketch out your ideas, and then build prototypes to help you test your assumptions and explore the problem in a different way. Seek out new options and eliminate old ones as you grow and evolve your understanding.

If this process becomes your new way of thinking and doing, you are on your way to shaping technologies that will make a real difference.

Recap of What You Need to Know

Finalizing the design:

- Following a UX process will give you confidence that your design is where it needs to be.

- How much documentation do you need? Just as much as makes sense to your personal situation. At a minimum, consider:

  - your interactive prototypes as a model of the design

  - visual and interactions guides

- Pilot test before launching is always useful, so look out for the following:

  - ability to complete common tasks

  - where users first click

  - interpretation of your content out of context

  - comprehension of your product and service information

  - what users value about your site

- evaluate the information and content priorities from the users' perspective

- check forms and the flow of these

- Simplify your design and remove items that you might have felt were immovable.

Uncover habits to change behavior:

- Iterate your design once you've launched, based on observation of users' behavior with your live product.

- Focus on the following factors before your site launches and validate once you've launched over time:

  - intrinsic value of your product

  - possible hurdles to overcome

  - how your product stacks up against competitors

  - what makes users become habitual users of your product

  - scalability and growth of your market

  - viability of your product once launched

- Understand what makes a habit and measure it once you have launched.

- Before launching, focus on expected measures:

  - define an habitual user

  - anticipate frequency of use

  - use the product yourself and consider your usage of it

  - focus on behavior first and data to assist understanding

- After launching, focus on measuring:

  - set a baseline

  - understand why people drop off

- crunch your numbers

- be patient

- Learn from your early adopters of the product and see how they use it in expected or unexpected ways.

- Model habitual users' behavior through:

  - data and analytics focus

  - UX processes and methods to uncover "why"

Final Word: the Rules of UX

Where to next? Get to work! Implement a UX process on your next project and reap the rewards. And remember:

- Keep challenging your process

- Think hard about who you involve

- Be user-centered

- Examine parallel situations

- Look to extreme users

- Consider the whole journey

- Prototype your design work

- Think stories as well as concepts

- Show your personality

- Launch to learn about behavior

- Seek direct user feedback rather than completely rely on data

- Iterate and modify your approach

- Stay positive!

Index

Thanks for buying this book. We really appreciate your support!

We'd like to think that you're now a "Friend of SitePoint," and so would like to invite you to our special "Friends of SitePoint" page.

Here you can SAVE up to 43% on a range of other super-cool SitePoint products.

Save over 40% with this link:

Link: 🌐 sitepoint.com/friends

Password: friends